RACIST LOGIC

MARKETS, DRUGS, SEX

Editors-in-Chief Deborah Chasman & Joshua Cohen

Executive Editor Chloe Fox

Managing Editor Adam McGee

Senior Editor Matt Lord

Engagement Editor Rosie Gillies

Editorial Assistants Anwar Omeish & Catherine Zhang

Publisher Louisa Daniels Kearney

Marketing and Development Manager Dan Manchon

Finance Manager Anthony DeMusis III

Distributor The MIT Press, Cambridge, Massachusetts,
and London, England

Printer Sheridan PA

Board of Advisors Derek Schrier (chairman), Archon Fung, Deborah
Fung, Alexandra Robert Gordon, Richard M. Locke, Jeff Mayersohn,
Jennifer Moses, Scott Nielsen, Robert Pollin, Rob Reich, Hiram Samel,
Kim Malone Scott

Interior Graphic Design Zak Jensen

Cover Design Alex Camlin

Racist Logic is *Boston Review* Forum 10 (44.2)

Peter James Hudson's essay "Bankers and Empire" is adapted and
reprinted with permission from *Bankers and Empire: How Wall Street
Colonized the Caribbean*, by Peter James Hudson, published by the
University of Chicago Press. © 2017 by the University of Chicago Press.
All rights reserved.

To become a member, visit:
bostonreview.net/membership/

For questions about donations and major gifts,
contact: Dan Manchon, dan@bostonreview.net

For questions about memberships, call 877-406-2443
or email Customer_Service@bostonreview.info.

Boston Review
PO Box 425786, Cambridge, MA 02142
617-324-1360

ISSN: 0734-2306 / ISBN: 978-1-946511-36-2

Editors' Note

Deborah Chasman & Joshua Cohen

WITH WHITE MORTALITY RATES soaring as a result of opioid use, drug addiction has morphed from a criminal crisis into a health crisis. This should not surprise us since, as Donna Murch notes in her lead essay, "Historically, the fundamental division between 'dope' and medicine was the race and class of users."

But by examining the opioid crisis alongside the War on Drugs— which has locked up so many people of color—as well as the Trump administration's immigration policies, Murch brings an otherwise familiar story into new territory. To understand the twisted logic that created the divergent responses to drug use—succor and sympathy for white users, prison and expulsion for people of color—Murch draws on Cedric Robinson's idea of racial capitalism. She shows how a racialized regime of drug prohibitions and a commercialized approach to prescription pharmaceuticals led Purdue Pharma to market OxyContin specifically to whites because it guaranteed them the longest head start on enforcement attempts and thus the biggest profits.

Racist Logic continues *Boston Review*'s interest in racial capitalism, and readers will find that it resonates with Forum 1, *Race Capitalism Justice*, to which Murch was also a contributor. Other contributors to *Racist Logic* consider how the idea of a specifically racial capitalism helps us understand the history of international banking (Peter James Hudson), the consumerism and commodification of black masculinity (Jordanna Matlon), the buying and selling of women's eggs and uteruses (Alys Eve Weinbaum), Michelle Obama's dubious bootstrap advice to black youth (Keeanga-Yamahtta Taylor), and the workings of affirmative action at elite universities (Richard Thomspon Ford).

The logic is grim, but there is cause for hope. As we go to press, a number of museums have announced that they will refuse money from the Sackler family, which owns Purdue Pharma—yielding, in part, to protests organized by forum respondent L.A. Kauffman. Moreover, the company settled a $270 million lawsuit with the state of Oklahoma, opening the door for future cases. Our ambitious hope is that *Racist Logic* will in some way contribute to this momentum.

Chasman & Cohen

How Race Made the Opioid Crisis

Donna Murch

IN MARCH 2018, President Donald Trump delivered a forty-minute speech about the crisis of addiction and overdose in New Hampshire. Standing before a wall tiled with the words "Opioids: The Crisis Next Door," Trump blankly recited the many contributors to the current drug epidemic, including doctors, dealers, and manufacturers. Trump droned on mechanically until he reached a venomous crescendo about Customs and Border Protection's seizure of 1,500 pounds of fentanyl. He brightened as he shifted focus to three of his most hated enemies, first blaming China and Mexico for saturating the United States with deadly synthetic opioids, then moving seamlessly to what he considered one of the great internal threats: "My administration is also confronting things called 'sanctuary cities,'" Trump declared. "Ending sanctuary cities is crucial to stopping the drug addiction crisis."

Like so many of Trump's proclamations, this rhetoric is sheer political fantasy.

Since the late 1990s, yearly rates of overdose deaths from legal "white market" opioids have consistently exceeded those from heroin. According to the Centers for Disease Control and Prevention, between 1999 and 2017, opioid overdoses killed nearly 400,000 people with 68 percent of those deaths linked to prescription medications. Moreover, as regulators and drug companies tightened controls on diversion and misuse after 2010, the American Society of Addiction Medicine determined that at least 80 percent of "new heroin users started out misusing prescription pain killers." Some data sets point to even higher numbers. In response to a 2014 survey of people undergoing treatments for opioid addiction, 94 percent of people surveyed said that they turned to heroin because prescription opioids were "far more expensive and harder to obtain."

In the face of these statistics, the claim that the opioid crisis is the product of Mexican and Central American migration—rather than the deregulation of Big Pharma and the failures of a private health care system—is not only absurd, but insidious. It substitutes racial myth for fact, thereby rationalizing an ever-expanding machinery of punishment while absolving one of the most lucrative, and politically influential, business lobbies in the United States. This paradoxical relationship between a racialized regime of illegal drug prohibition and a highly commercial, laissez-faire approach to prescription pharmaceuticals cannot be understood without recourse to how racial capitalism has structured pharmacological markets throughout U.S. history. The linguistic convention of "white" and "black" markets points to how steeped our ideas of licit and illicit are in the metalanguage of race.

Historically, the fundamental division between "dope" and medicine was the race and class of users. The earliest salvos in the U.S. domestic drug wars can be traced to anti-opium ordinances in late nineteenth-century

California as Chinese laborers poured into the state during the railroad building boom. In 1914 the federal government passed the Harrison Narcotics Act, which taxed and regulated opiates and coca products. Similarly, as rates of immigration increased in the aftermath of the Mexican revolution, Congress passed the Marijuana Tax Act of 1937, which targeted the customs and culture of newly settled migrants. Although "cannabis" was well known in the United States—it was used in numerous tinctures and medicines—a racial scare campaign swept the country and warned that "marijuana" aroused men of color's violent lust for white women.

As bad as the early drug panics were, they paled in comparison to the carceral regime of drug prohibition and policing that emerged in the years after the civil rights movement. In the 1980s and 1990s, mass incarceration and the overlapping War(s) on Drugs and Gangs became de facto urban policy for impoverished communities of color in U.S. cities. Legislation expanded state and federal mandatory minimums for drug offenses, denied public housing to entire families if any member was even suspected of a drug crime, lengthened the list of crimes eligible for the federal death penalty, and imposed draconian restrictions of parole. Ultimately, multiple generations of youth of color found themselves confined under long prison sentences and faced with lifelong social and economic marginality.

Today, much of the Trump administration's rhetoric is taken from decades of drug and incarceration frenzies past, including the threat of the death penalty for drug trafficking (Bill Clinton), Just Say No campaigns (Ronald Reagan), and the reinvigoration of the War on Gangs (Bill Clinton again). "We are all facing a deadly lucrative international drug trade," warned Trump's then attorney general, Jeff Sessions. As he spoke before the International Association of Chiefs of Police in the fall of 2017, Sessions laid out a law-and-order platform that promised to "back the blue," reduce crime, and dismantle "transnational criminal organizations." He drew so heavily from 1980s anti-drug hysteria, in fact, that he earned giddy praise from Edwin Meese III, Reagan's attorney general who helped enshrined the 100-to-1 sentencing disparity between crack and powder cocaine. "Largely unnoticed has been the extraordinary work that . . . Sessions has done in the Department of Justice to create a Reaganesque resurgence of law and order," Meese opined in *USA Today* in January 2018.

Over the past two years, Trump and Sessions repeatedly used the threat of drugs and racial contagion for a reactionary portfolio ranging from reversals of modest criminal justice reforms of the Obama era—including reinstating federal civil forfeiture, limiting federal power to implement consent decrees at the local level, and the expansion of mandatory minimum sentencing in the federal system—to the building of a wall along the Mexican border. And, although anti-crime rhetoric no longer has the same purchase as it did in the era of Willie Horton or Ricky Ray Rector—thanks in large part to activist efforts to delegitimize mass incarceration—the reinvigorated machinery of criminalization remains firmly in place.

Integrating the opioid crisis with the War on Drugs raises questions beyond familiar narratives and political discourses. In the United States, prohibition of illicit drugs and the mass marketing of licit pharmaceuticals fit together in a larger framework of racial capitalism and deregulation that are deeply intertwined and mutually reinforcing. The opioid crisis would not have been possible without the racial regimes that have long structured both illicit and licit modes of consumption. As we will see, the demonization of urban, nonwhite drug users played a crucial role in the opening of "white" pharmaceutical markets in the 1990s that proved so enormously profitable to companies such as Purdue Pharma and paved the way for our current public health crisis.

IN THE 1990s, Purdue created aggressive marketing campaigns to convince doctors and state regulators of the safety of a new class of timed-release opioid analgesics. Given their status as Schedule II controlled substances, Purdue faced potentially enormous pushback, especially at a time when the number of people incarcerated for drug offenses was reaching an all-time high. However, a major shift had taken place in regulatory policy a decade before that made this possible. In the 1980s, President Reagan initiated a radical program of corporate deregulation that opened the door to a new era of pharmaceutical mass marketing. Reagan's "Second American Revolution" slashed government oversight, pushed through expedited review by the Food and Drug Administration (FDA), and for the first time allowed direct-to-consumer advertising for pharmaceutical drugs.

Amazingly, the deregulation of Big Pharma took place while the Reagan administration was launching a bombastic "second" War on Drugs that established a new standard for illicit drug prohibition, one his successors George H. W. Bush and Bill Clinton not only met but exceeded. This potent mix of racialized drug prosecution and corporate empowerment created the environment in which Purdue and other companies sought out new commercial strategies for marketing opioids.

So when Purdue introduced OxyContin in 1996, it proceeded with an awareness of both the opportunities and potential pitfalls. The company developed a number of marketing strategies to increase sales *and* to navigate the deeply segregated waters of drug consumption. In order to market OxyContin, a long-term release opioid that contains the active ingredient oxycodone, Purdue created an expansive network of sales representatives, doubling its internal sales force from 318 in 1996 to 671 in 2000. Driven by sophisticated data collection methods that revealed the highest and lowest prescribers in every zip code throughout the United States, Purdue identified medical practices with the largest numbers of pain patients and with physicians who were the least discriminate prescribers. Sales representatives received bonuses ranging from $15,000 to $240,000 a year for increases in opioid prescriptions in their coverage areas, and they visited doctors repeatedly, drawing them into an elaborate informational marketing campaign. Purdue offered doctors educational conferences in Sunbelt resorts, patient coupons, OxyContin-branded stuffed animals, and even CDs of the drug's marketing jingle, "Get in the Swing of OxyContin."

The company's aggressive sales tactics convinced primary care physicians (PCPs) to prescribe opioids much more frequently for a wide range of patient complaints, including lower back pain and arthritis. By 2003 PCPs made up nearly half of OxyContin prescribers. Some experts at the time worried that PCPs lacked independent training in chronic pain management and addiction. Meanwhile the increase in the sale of OxyContin—from $48 million upon its introduction to $1.1 billion four years later—demonstrates the enormous scale of this enterprise.

According to public health scholars Helena Hansen and Julie Netherland, Purdue's success hinged not only on this aggressive sales campaign, but also on racially bifurcated understandings of addiction. Drug sales representatives directed advertisement to overwhelmingly white suburban and rural areas to avoid the stigma of racially coded urban drug markets. By crafting a geographically distinct, white consumer base—understood as the antithesis of "hardcore" (nonwhite) urban drug users targeted by the Wars on Drugs and Gangs—the company both benefitted from and reinforced the racial ideology underwriting these punitive campaigns.

Not surprisingly, the regions that initially showed the highest rates of opioid abuse in the early 2000s—including rural Maine, West Virginia, Kentucky, and western Pennsylvania—had overwhelmingly white populations. Although the press termed OxyContin "hillbilly heroin" and the drug of choice for poor whites, public health researchers have shown that affluent suburbanites also had high rates of abuse, exemplified by Rush Limbaugh's disclosure of his own prescription opioid abuse in 2003. Racial disparities in health care access, discriminatory prescribing patterns among physicians, and a self-conscious strategy by pharmaceutical companies that cultivated "legitimate" white consumer markets all contributed to the racial demographics of the opioid crisis.

A key reason that pharmaceutical companies could market such a powerful sustained release analgesic to treat "non-malignant pain" was that they made assumptions about their intended consumers. "The disproportionate uptake of OxyContin by rural and suburban prescribers in majority white states (Maine, Kentucky and West Virginia) is notable in light of the historical hostility of regulatory agencies such as the DEA to the expansion of opioid use," argue Hansen and Netherland. "Urban markets would have brought with them race and class imagery of illicit use that may have made expanded prescription of OxyContin for moderate pain a hard sell to regulators."

In a similar line of analysis, pharmaceutical historian David Herzberg, author of *Happy Pills in America: From Miltown to Prozac* (2009), places the opioid crisis in the larger sweep of U.S. history. According to Herzberg, there is no real difference between prescription medicines and illicit drugs. Both possess physical and psychoactive effects, but the social meaning attributed to them has more to do with race, class, and differential application of state power than pharmacology. The contemporary disparity between licit and illicit has its origins in the

Jim Crow era, when the Supreme Court back the principle of separate but equal. In the years after World War II, the civil rights movement challenged racial discrimination in consumer markets, rendering illegal the most overt forms of discrimination, such as segregated lunch counters, public conveyances, and housing covenants. But the racialized division between licit and illicit drug markets endured. Indeed, it provides a primary rationale for the Wars on Drugs and Crime that emerged after the Voting Rights Act. Today African Americans and Latinos make up 80 percent of those incarcerated in federal prisons for drug crimes and 60 percent of those in state prisons.

One of the most compelling aspects of Herzberg's analysis is his historical exploration of how postwar white consumers defined themselves against racially coded, urban drug users by redefining pharmacological relief as an entitlement. In the same period that Richard Nixon launched the first War on Drugs, white consumers steeped in the discourse of the silent majority demanded access to pharmaceuticals as a citizenship right. "I, as one American citizen make demand at this writing to restore all the drugs that people need," argued a complaint to the FDA. "Too many people are suffering and being penalized on account of the drug abusers."

This "problematic social entitlement" functioned as the flip side of the more familiar story of criminalization and divestment of black and brown populations in the Wars on Drugs and Crime. Prohibition of urban vice required a space of white absolution that enabled the profitable mass-marketing of licit pharmaceuticals. "A focus on pharmaceutical white markets tells a very different story: of a divided system of drug control designed to encourage and enable a segregated market for psychoactive substances," Herzberg argues. "This regime established a privilege—maximal freedom of rational choice in a relatively safe drug market . . . and linked this privilege both institutionally and culturally to social factors such as economic class and whiteness."

Cultural logics, as well as criminal justice policy, have also reinforced and animated the racialized boundary between "licit health seekers" and "illicit pleasure seekers" in the popular imagination. Iconic drug films such as *Traffic* (2000) and *Requiem for a Dream* (2000) dramatize the tragedy of white women's descent into illegal narcotic use through pornographic narratives in which "innocent" young white girls are coerced into interracial sex by black male "pushers." Drawing on the cinematic grammar of D. W. Griffith's classic KKK paean *Birth of a Nation* (1915), they reenact the white supremacist ideology that reinforced racial segregation. Viewed in this way, the opioid crisis appears not as an unprecedented phenomenon, but the product of longstanding historical processes.

The role of white absolution is even clearer when looking at the disparate consequences for illicit drug use across the color line. Nothing speaks more profoundly to how the state artificially constructed segregated drug markets than federal prosecutions for crack use. Few realize that almost no white people were ever charged with crack offenses by federal authorities. This is despite the federal government's own data from the National Institute of Drug Abuse (NIDA) documenting that over two-thirds of crack users were white. Between 1986, when Congress signed the Anti-Drug Abuse Act into law, and 1994, when President Clinton's crime bill was passed, not a single white person was convicted of a federal crack offense in Miami, Boston, Denver, Chicago, Dallas, or Los Angeles. "Out of hundreds of cases, only one white was convicted in California, two in Texas, three in New York and two in Pennsylvania," noted *Los Angeles Times* reporter Dan Weikel. Instead, prosecutors shunted their cases into the state system, which had much lower rates of conviction and shorter sentences.

AT THE HEART of this disparity is the paradoxical relationship in the United States between prohibition and provision: some of the harshest advocates for punishment and the criminalization of illicit drug use have also enthusiastically supported and defended pharmaceutical deregulation and expanded access to opioids. If there is any doubt about Trump's acquiescence to Big Pharma—despite his campaign promises to lower Medicare drug prices—one need look no further than his appointment of Alex Azar II, former president of the U.S. division of pharmaceutical giant Eli Lilly and Co., to serve as secretary of health and human services.

The career of Rudolph Giuliani is one of the best examples of this cognitive dissonance around drug policy that can only properly be understood as a product of racial capitalism. As mayor of New York (1994–2001), Giuliani and his police commissioner, William Bratton, were central architects of the city's zero tolerance, quality-of-life policing, which criminalized low-level offenses ranging from panhandling and graffiti to illegal vending and minor cannabis possession. Giuliani's administration presided over about 40,000 marijuana arrests per year, up nearly fortyfold from earlier decades. In fact, the highest number of marijuana possession arrests ever recorded in New York City took place under the Giuliani administration, with 51,267 arrests in the year 2000. Giuliani also led a vicious campaign against methadone treatment in the 1990s, advocating complete abstinence as the only acceptable response to illicit drugs.

Given his hardline stance on drug prohibition, it is striking that two years after New York's all-time high for marijuana arrests, the former New York mayor and prosecutor took on Purdue Pharma as a client, agreeing to help the company fend off a federal investigation into improper marketing of OxyContin. "There are tens of millions of Americans suffering from persistent pain," argued Giuliani. "We must find a way to ensure access to appropriate prescription pain medications for those suffering from the debilitating effects of pain while working to prevent the abuse and diversion of these same vital medicines."

John Brownlee, a U.S. attorney from the western district of Virginia, initiated the investigation into Purdue Pharma shortly after his federal appointment in response to skyrocketing numbers of opioid overdoses in his region. "This was pushed by the company to be marketed in an illegal way, pushed from the highest levels of the company, that in my view made them a criminal enterprise that needed to be dealt with," Brownlee explained. Although the young attorney's legal action was the first successful criminal suit against Purdue, the company currently faces a number of civil suits from other states, including Texas, New York, Indiana, and Massachusetts. (Already, in March, it agreed to a $270 million settlement with the state of Oklahoma.)

In the Viriginia case, Giuliani provided Purdue with legal services as well as access to his extensive network of political connections in Washington. He finessed an agreement that kept senior executives from serving prison time and attempted to restrict future prosecution of Purdue. According to the *Guardian*, Giuliani's intervention avoided "a bar on Purdue doing business with the federal government which would have killed a large part of the multibillion-dollar market for the drug."

ACTIVISTS, investigative journalists, and public sector attorneys have produced a significant body of work documenting the culpability of pharmaceutical companies in the contemporary opioid crisis. Until quite recently, however, this history has largely failed to penetrate mainstream opinion. Despite the pathbreaking investigative journalism of Barry Meier's *Pain Killer* (2003) and Chris McGreal's *American Overdose* (2018), popular exposés have frequently centered on unethical practices by individual doctors and "pill mills," rather than excavating how Purdue and other companies built a commercial infrastructure that revolutionized narcotics sale at enormous social cost. Culpability is shared by a resource-starved FDA and regulatory infrastructure's failure to intervene when it became apparent that widespread abuse was taking place. Unfortunately, the young have been the hardest hit. The *New York Times* recently estimated that nearly 400,000 people currently addicted to prescription opioids or heroin are between 18 and 25 years old. Even more troubling is that in states such as Ohio and West Virginia with the highest rates of prescription opioid consumption, 50–80 percent of foster care placements are linked to substance abuse in the home. In the realm of health and human pain, free market fundamentalism has proved quite deadly.

The origins of the opioid crisis in the licit pharmaceutical market calls not only for a rethinking of the politics of deregulation, but also an end to the sclerotic, racialized War on Drugs narrative still mobilized by the Trump administration. In moving testimony before the House Judiciary Committee on Immigration and Border Security, Stanford psychologist and West Virginia native Keith Humphreys spoke directly to this issue in February 2018:

> West Virginia is emblematic of where this epidemic is at its most destructive —rural areas that don't have sanctuary cities and indeed generally don't have cities at all. Recent immigrants are rare, yet opioid addiction is rampant. That's because the opioid epidemic was made in America, not in Mexico, China, or any other foreign country. . . . The astonishing increase in providing opioids—which at its apex reached nearly a quarter billion

prescriptions per year—is what started and still maintains our opioid epidemic. Prescription opioids come from American companies and are prescribed by American doctors overseen by American regulators.

Like many crises, our current dilemma also presents opportunities to radically rethink our approaches to both prohibition and provision. In addition to recognizing the role of Big Pharma, a critical look at the opioid crisis also requires examining the larger environment in which this predatory marketing campaign took place. Structural issues of economic downward mobility, diminished occupational safety and health protections, lack of health care access, and the limitations of managed care have all contributed.

Critically, we must push back against the racist logic that has long underwritten prohibition efforts while occluding, and even assisting, the pharmaceutical industry's attempt to expand its reach. Phantasms of drug sale and consumption continue to animate deeply felt national narratives demarcating the line between white and black, native and foreign, innocent and guilty, medical and recreational, deserving and undeserving, licit and illicit. The Trump administration, like its Democratic and Republican predecessors, has drawn some of its most destructive symbols of racial animus from the War on Drugs repertoire. One of the most important lessons to be learned from viewing the opioid crisis and War on Drugs through the lens of racial capitalism is that the privileges of whiteness come at a great social cost, not only for those excluded from them, but also for those who possess them. As our nation witnesses a significant drop in life expectancy due to high rates of suicide and overdose, an honest reckoning with the true nature of power and culpability in the United States has never been more urgent.

Race and the First Opium Crisis

Max Mishler

FOLLOWING THE RACIST LOGIC Donna Murch exposes in the contemporary opioid crisis leads back to the nineteenth century. The Sackler family, which owns Purdue Pharma, is neither the first drug cartel to capture wealth by pushing opium on a vulnerable population nor the only one to sanitize profits through philanthropic donations.

Consider the following example. The Boston merchant Thomas Handasyd Perkins profited handsomely from the Atlantic slave trade, but like many others, he gradually turned his attention to opium and amassed a fortune. His nephew and fellow cartel member, John Murray Forbes (of the storied Forbes family), used ill-gotten drug loot to become the country's earliest railroad magnate. These captains of industry were, of course, nothing if not considerate of their fellow man. Perkins used his drug money to establish hospitals, schools, and libraries throughout the Boston area, while Forbes became an ardent abolitionist, financing the free-staters in Kansas during the 1850s and working tirelessly on behalf of Abraham Lincoln's presidential campaign in 1860 and 1864. Slave trading and drug pushing thus helped subsidize northern humanitarianism.

Perkins and Forbes provide useful entry points for reconstructing a larger, global story of what we might call the long Opium Wars.

BUILDING ON the pioneering work of Caribbean scholar-activist Eric Williams, a new generation of U.S. historians emphasizes the centrality of slavery to U.S. and British economic development. As these scholars have shown, a sophisticated "empire of cotton" linked enslaved cotton pickers in Mississippi to cotton brokers in New York and Liverpool, cotton manufacturers in Lowell and Manchester, and bankers throughout the Anglo-American world. No slavery, no cotton; no cotton, no industrial revolution; no industrial revolution, no Anglo-American economic supremacy, so the story goes. Yet despite scholar Lisa Lowe's call to consider the "intimacies of four continents," South and East Asia have remained curiously marginal to this Atlantic story. One of the most important engines of cotton capitalism, however, was the opium trade to China.

From the time Christopher Columbus first set sail, China had been the ultimate prize—a real commercial El Dorado stimulating Euro-American libidinal economic fantasies. Europeans spoke of conquest, but China remained independent and controlled the terms of trade. In fact, the majority of silver pilfered from the Americas during the sixteenth, seventeenth, and eighteenth centuries found its way to China, which needed relatively little from Europe but had much to offer (tea, silk, and spices). Opium was one potential solution to this massive trade imbalance that inhibited early industrialization. Importing a highly addictive commodity proved to be the most important tool for British and U.S. merchants eager to rearrange the China trade on favorable terms. When Chinese authorities responded by prohibiting opium imports around 1800, an illicit drug trade was born that escalated into a series of opium rushes, transforming Western opium smugglers into capitalist pioneers and buttressing British imperialism in Asia.

By the 1820s, opium was the single greatest Western import into China. While the British East India Company controlled 90 percent of the opium trade, thanks to its monopoly on Indian-grown opium, U.S. firms cornered the market on smuggling a cheaper Turkish product into China—prospering by selling death and despair. "Opium was more than simply an economic commodity," Lowe notes. "The distribution of the highly addicting drug that induced docility and dependence targeted the biology of the Chinese population, constituting a very different form of governance than earlier modes of political dominance or territorial conquest." The opium peddler, claimed British reformers, "slays the body after he has corrupted, degraded and annihilated the moral being of unhappy sinners."

Opium smuggling served larger imperial goals in addition to generating outrageous profits. While Liverpool cotton brokers successfully married British industrial capitalism to what historian Walter Johnson has called "slave-racial capitalism" in the U.S. South, manufacturers in cities such as Manchester quickly pushed domestic consumption to its limits and became desperate for new markets that could absorb surplus product and forestall recessions. Many capitalists pinned their hopes on India and China, home to the largest reserve army of consumers on Earth. But neither Indian nor Chinese peasants had much use for European manufactures. Instead, British narco-colonialism opened up new markets—that is, newly conquered consumers—for a different product: opium. These markets were predicated on the coerced cultivation of opium in India and its coerced consumption in China.

When Chinese authorities once again targeted opium smuggling in the 1830s, the British responded with all-out war—two, in fact

(1839–42 and 1856–60). Imperial violence against China complemented the torture of enslaved blacks on cotton plantations in the West, forming a global regime of racial capitalism. Abolitionists, meanwhile, drew explicit connections between the suffering of enslaved blacks and Chinese opium addicts, both of whom were vulnerable racialized populations subjected to the depredations of Anglo-American capitalism. The Irish abolitionist Richard Allen, for example, was a persistent advocate for "the prisoned, plundered Chinese, whom the English are warring against, in the hope of making them swallow opium . . . the Hindoos, who are forced to grow the opium, and taxed for the support of Juggernaut . . . American slaves, and slaves everywhere."

The U.S. Civil War temporarily disrupted the cotton economy, but racial capitalism proved flexible enough to survive the abolition of slavery. As for Britain, its victory in the Second Opium War resulted not only in the complete legalization of the opium trade but also in the consolidation of the Chinese "coolie trade." Both countries saw domestic opium consumption skyrocket. In the United States, opium and opioid derivatives distributed to sick and wounded soldiers during the Civil War made opium the first mass-consumption narcotic in U.S. history. The negative connotations of opium use, however, were reserved for Chinese immigrants rather than veterans or middle-class white women addicted to morphine. As the historian David Courtright shows, transformations in medical practice as well as racial and class anxieties eventually led to legislation such as the 1914 Harrison Narcotics Tax Act that produced illegal drug markets and immoral (i.e., working-class and nonwhite) drug users.

The turn of the twentieth century witnessed a series of racial panics that trafficked in the grammar of addiction. Racist depictions of Chinese opium use underscored the Chinese threat to U.S. society and bolstered racist political campaigns for Chinese exclusion during the 1880s and 1890s. Meanwhile, black resistance to racial terror was interpreted through the lens of "Negro cocaine madness." By the 1930s, in response to Mexican immigration and Latinx urbanization, white observers worried about "reefer madness." In each case, white drug addiction was bracketed amid increased concern about racialized laboring populations whose indocility justified what Micol Seigel calls the "violence work" of policing. These moral panics veiled the fact that early giants of the pharmaceutical industry—Bayer and Merck—amassed fortunes producing heroin, cocaine, and methamphetamines for citizens and soldiers.

NINETEENTH-CENTURY REGIMES of racial narco-capitalism thus haunt the opioid crisis of today. They remind us that domestic U.S. opioid consumption is only one side of a global story. Trump's obscene attempts to blame Latinx immigrants for the United States' nasty habit must not obscure the role of U.S. imperialism in transforming Afghanistan into a narco-state that supplies a majority of the world's illicit opium (including a significant amount that finds its way onto U.S. streets, where users without prescriptions turn to illicit substitutes). The Sacklers are only one face of contemporary racial narco-capitalism, which keeps universities, hospitals, and philanthropic foundations flush with drug money.

The only way to escape the corrupting influence of capital derived from slavery and the long Opium Wars is to wage a global struggle, as our abolitionist forebears did, against racial tyranny and economic plunder.

Black Drugs, White Drugs

Britt Rusert

DONNA MURCH SHOWS that we continue to live in a world made by Reagan, one where corporate empowerment both benefits from and reinforces racialized regimes of punishment. In this smoke-and-mirrors theater of national distraction, nonwhite populations are stereotyped, locked up, and otherwise sacrificed so that corporate exploitation and dispossession can proceed apace, behind closed doors and beyond the reach of public accountability. Trump thus represents only the most recent—and chaotic—outbreak of a much longer epidemic of racial capitalism. His public speeches often sound like a hallucinatory rehash of sound bites from the history of U.S. conservatism, parroting the racist drug policy and rhetoric of earlier administrations. The age of Trump is thus an age of unveiling: his language blatantly exposes the usually unstated logic of state violence and its predation on vulnerable populations in the name of corporate theft, capitalist accumulation, and widening social immiseration and dispossession.

Murch gives the example of Purdue Pharma's OxyContin market strategy, which sought to avoid the PR and regulatory stigmas of being associated with "urban" (black) drug users. The result was a white market that took shape through aggressive marketing campaigns and targeting of states with majority white populations that were also known for their hostility to federal regulation. Thus the "white drug" was born. There is also the racialization of the crisis itself, which Murch does not discuss: the suffering and deaths of nonwhite users are virtually invisible, obscured by a discourse focused on saving innocent white users from harm. Purdue's consumer strategy thus produced two dynamics: a market of control, in which white patients in pain became addicted to opioids, and a market of abandonment, in which black pain is ignored.

In addition to being a site of profound injustice and a political wedge issue, race thus became a strategy for market expansion. But the racialization of pharmaceuticals runs deeper than appeals to whiteness; blackness, too, has become a source of Big Pharma profit extraction. In 2005 a company named NitroMed used a strategy similar to Purdue's when it gained approval for a heart-failure medication that was specially targeted to African American patients. After the drug, BiDil, was initially rejected by the FDA in 1997, researchers sought to resuscitate it as a racial medicine by seizing on data from the original clinical trials to argue that black patients responded better to the drug than white patients. The first FDA-approved drug with a race-specific indication, BiDil was approved and marketed as a "black drug," despite limited and unconvincing evidence that race played any role in the drug's effectiveness.

The story of BiDil adds one more twist to the story Murch exposes of a segregated pharmaceutical market. NitroMed's marketing campaign targeted black consumers through grassroots networks and African American community spaces, including schools, community centers, radio, and churches. Murch notes that desegregation did not extend to medical care or the racial structuring of drug markets, but BiDil reminds us that drug makers have occasionally deployed the language and social capital of civil rights to sell racial drugs.

BiDil also points to a time when drug makers tried and failed to target black patients. An expensive and unnecessary repackaging of two generics already on the market, BiDil failed and NitroMed folded in 2009. But in a capitalist system, failed drugs often denote merely failed business models: they stand ready to be pulled back into cycles of market acquisition and rebranding. BiDil itself is a case in point; it was bought by the Atlanta-based company, Arbor Pharmaceuticals, which the very day I write this announced the launch of the "Shaquille Gets Real About Heart Failure" campaign, teaming up with basketball superstar Shaquille O'Neal to resuscitate what has been called a "controversial and spectacularly unsuccessful cardiology drug." The strategy is ubiquitous. In her study of how Big Pharma's flight from Nigeria has profoundly shaped both legal and illegal drug economies there (as well as stoked cultural anxieties about unsafe and "fake" drugs), anthropologist Kristin Peterson writes about the significant ontological confusion that surrounds drugs today—about the actual composition of drugs as well as the legality of their circulation—which pharmaceutical companies exploit for profit. The ongoing War on Drugs also depends on this categorical fuzziness to bend drug policy to the needs and desires of the racial state.

Perhaps most chilling about the NitroMed story is the company's cynical manipulation of the history of racism, which portrayed BiDil as the cure to generations of health disparities. In this, it also pulls back the curtain on an insidious technique of racial capitalism: appropriate injustice in order to sell products and capture profits. In NitroMed's case, the long and brutal legacy of medical neglect and exploitation—with roots going back to the Atlantic slave trade—was remade into a marketing ploy. (One thinks as well of Ram Trucks' commercial during the 2018 Super Bowl, which featured a speech of Martin Luther King, Jr.)

NitroMed's marketing was exploitative not only because of the high cost of the drug but also because selling it would only empower the social structures—including rampant corporate power, a broken insurance system, and a privatized, neoliberal health care regime—that helped to cause the racial health disparities in the first place. In this sense, no drug, no matter how miraculous, can ever hope to remedy the root causes of racial injustice. Indeed, in the case of OxyContin, a drug only further exacerbated them. Murch shows that racial capitalism can have damaging effects that radiate far beyond those specifically targeted as patients and consumers.

The pattern of profiting from racialized sickness endures, and it shows no sign of stopping. In the wake of the opioid crisis, whiteness is becoming more and more visible as a site of medical intervention; it can now be deployed as a category for drug marketing in a way that would have been impossible in the past. One reason is the negative health outcomes increasingly associated with whiteness itself, including higher suicide rates, reduced life expectancy, and the deleterious health effects of racial resentment chronicled by Jonathan Metzl in his book *Dying of Whiteness* (2019). Another is the resurgence of cultural anxieties—facilitated by Trump and undergirded by a eugenic logic of whiteness—about demographic change, what philosopher Achille Mbembe has called the "becoming black of the world."

Murch shows clearly how our society is calibrated toward the health of markets rather than the health of people. As the story of BiDil teaches us, we cannot expect a market solution to solve this problem. Correcting the imbalance will require challenging entrenched corporate power and the Reagan-era logic of markets—both of abandonment and of control—head on. It may also require more utopian strategies, including imagining a world in which medications are not commodities at all.

The Cure Amplifies the Problem

Helena Hansen, Julie Netherland,

& David Herzberg

DONNA MURCH's masterful description of the roots of the opioid crisis coheres with our study of corporate pharmaceutical executives, addiction researchers, and medical practitioners. We too find that racial capital has played a central role in creating the "white" overdose epidemic through drug regulation, drug marketing, and law enforcement. Racial parsing has meant that even while pharmaceutical opioid markets grew out of control, drug-war style law enforcement continued to inflict its devastating harms, especially in black and brown communities.

But Big Pharma's carefully constructed racial capital did not end with the *creation* of the opioid crisis; it endures in the U.S. national *response*. Many of the same players now reap profits from treatments for the opioid dependence they helped to create. And the structures of access are marked by many of the same racial privileges.

Our current research, as documented in our forthcoming book, exposes and pushes back against this newest incarnation of the racial capital encoded into pharmaceutical markets. We focus on the central difference between U.S. drug policy before and after the "white" opioid crisis: a new emphasis on clinical treatment as opposed to punishment, and, especially, on pharmaceutical maintenance with medication-assisted treatment (MAT). The expansion of MAT is laudable in many ways, but it poses new problems of its own.

Buprenorphine, itself an opioid and the primary medication being promoted for MAT, was developed in the 1990s as a treatment for opioid dependence and was federally deregulated so that it could be prescribed in doctors' offices for use at home. This marked a radical departure from the stigmatized and tightly policed MAT traditionally provided in methadone clinics. Rather than being narrated as standard medical progress, however, this shift was narrated as the development of a treatment style appropriate for white people. As one official told Congress, methadone clinics "[tend] to be concentrated in urban areas" and "[are] a poor fit for the suburban spread of narcotic addiction" among "citizens who would not ordinarily be associated with the term addiction." Deregulating buprenorphine was necessary, in other words, because methadone was seen as inappropriate for white clients. Unsurprisingly, access to buprenorphine through private-practice physicians has been profoundly disparate along racial, economic, and geographic lines.

Unequal access is not the only way racial capital functions in the buprenorphine-centric response to the opioid crisis. The U.S. federal opioid plan—as articulated in Trump's opioid commission report, the 21st Century CURES Act of Congress, and the National Institutes of Health (NIH) HEAL initiative that it funds—emphasizes primary care–based expansion of MAT, largely buprenorphine maintenance. Related legislation has streamlined new drug approvals, reduced the FDA's review process for new drugs, and provided major NIH funding for public-private drug development partnerships and clinical trials. Prioritizing individual-level treatment, these policies give short shrift to health infrastructure development or social intervention while offering a bonanza to pharmaceutical companies. There is little to no funding specifically focused on marginalized groups (as defined by race, class, gender, LGTBQ status). There is equally little for the health care access, social services, and economic supports (such as housing) that have been shown in prior studies of opioid dependence and of analogous epidemics (such as HIV) to be critical to the success of pharmaceutical treatments.

Racial capital has so greatly warped our engagement with the opioid crisis that we are at grave risk of missing a new phase of the crisis even as its harms grow. For example, while attention has been focused on deaths among whites, deaths among blacks have been rising steadily. In 2012 blacks made up 7 percent of opioid overdose deaths; in 2017 that number rose to 12 percent. An analysis of 2017 overdose death data in New York City revealed that, for the first time in eleven years, compared with whites and Latinos, black New Yorkers had the highest rate of drug overdose deaths.

In this New York is not alone: according to data from the Centers for Disease Control, blacks in urban areas across the country have seen the sharpest increase in overdose deaths in recent years, driven largely by fentanyl in the drug supply. Yet we have not seen the same kind of media attention we saw for increases in overdose deaths among whites. Nor have we seen the humanizing depictions of black opioid users that now frame whites struggling with opioids as blameless, with tragically wasted talents and with loving families. Thus, even as white racial capital helped produce the opioid crisis, it also threatens to limit any hard-won progress—including low-barrier access to buprenorphine—along lines of race and class.

In fact, quite the opposite: despite the well-funded emphasis on MAT, we have seen no corresponding effort to dismantle the punitive drug war apparatus that has historically been responsible for caging millions of black and brown people. In the past decade, arrests for drug violations have actually increased by 3.2 percent. Prosecutors, politicians, and the public have called for an increase in so-called drug-induced homicide prosecutions. A Drug Policy Alliance report on overdosing reported that "in 2017 alone, elected officials in at least thirteen states introduced bills to create new drug-induced homicide offenses or strengthen existing drug-induced homicide laws." Although purportedly aimed at high-level drug manufacturers and distributors, analyses find that these prosecutions are most often leveled against friends of the descedents who were not selling significant quantities of drugs.

This criminalization is also spreading to rural areas and encompassing poor whites as well as people of color. An analysis of jail data suggests that in the past several years, jail populations have continued to grow larger in rural counties while they have declined in many large cities. Between 2004 and 2014, the percentage of white people in jail grew 19 percent in rural counties and 15 percent in small- and medium-sized cities. The focus on therapeutic responses to addiction for affluent and middle-class whites has not diminished punitive responses for black and Latinx as well as poor white people.

For all these reasons, MAT alone cannot solve the opioid crisis. In a nation that has relied heavily on pharmaceuticals to solve everything from depression to erectile dysfunction, the notion of a simplistic magic bullet and technological solution to the complex social problem of drug use is culturally compelling. But until we address the root causes of problematic opioid use—including the racial capital that has warped our governance of markets for psychoactive substances—MAT alone is unlikely to succeed. We need also to address a lack of basic needs such as housing and income, as well as the social isolation and stigma that exacerbate use, especially in economically depressed communities. In the United States, of course, all of these are deeply rooted in structural inequalities of race and class.

The opioid crisis is emblematic of larger shortcomings of the U.S. approach to complex public health and social problems. As such, it provides a singular opportunity to address those shortcomings in our public health and social infrastructures. What the crisis has revealed, among other things, is our tendency to subsidize corporate systems of racial capital while—partially as a consequence—failing to invest in public health and health care systems, particularly in low-income communities and communities of color. Now is the time to leverage political awareness to create a meaningful anti-racist campaign for change.

Hansen, Netherland, & Herzberg

No Gentler War on Drugs

Michael Collins

DONNA MURCH IS RIGHT that the rhetoric on drugs has softened along racial lines. The dominant narrative now mostly describes working-class white victims in rural states, despite recent data showing that drug death rates are rising sharply for African Americans. Prior drug "crises," such as those involving crack and heroin, were seen as inner-city issues that exclusively affected people of color, who were rarely extended the moral purity of victimhood. This racial transformation has led lawmakers, law enforcement, and mainstream media alike to display more compassion toward people who use drugs, as exemplified by the 2015 *New York Times* headline "White Families Seek Gentler War on Drugs." Yet public policies have not matched the rhetoric. Although in some cases we have moved toward a more health-centered approach to the overdose crisis, the rhetoric of compassion belies an ongoing and insidious entanglement with capitalism.

It is true that the government's response to the opioid epidemic has differed markedly from earlier drug panics. Traditional upticks in drug use—whether crack in the 1980s or methamphetamine in the

1990s—were met (under the Reagan, Clinton, and both Bush administrations) with an enforcement-centered response: tougher sentences, narcotic task forces, more prisons and law enforcement funding. The overdose crisis, by contrast, has led lawmakers to call for compassion and treatment. Under Obama, Congress passed legislation aimed at tackling the overdose crisis with a public health focus. Both the Comprehensive Addiction and Recovery Act and the 21st Century Cures Act, passed in 2016, poured billions of dollars into treatment. But beneath this compassionate approach, many of the quintessential characteristics of the drug war persist—fueled by money and power, not evidence.

Medication-assisted treatment (MAT) is a case in point. Despite overwhelming evidence for the efficacy of methadone and buprenorphine, the gold standard treatments for opioid use disorders, the government still fails when it comes to following the research. Both treatment options have decades of evidence demonstrating their effectiveness in reducing overdose deaths, yet they are increasingly superseded by a third medication for opioid use disorder, naltrexone. This drug's domination of the addiction field in recent years is partly driven by money.

According to the *New York Times*, the company that manufactures the drug under the brand name Vivitrol "has spent millions of dollars on contributions to officials struggling to stem the epidemic of opioid abuse. It has also provided thousands of free doses to encourage the use of Vivitrol in jails and prisons, which have by default become major detox centers." Unlike methadone and buprenorphine, which are carefully regulated opioids, Vivitrol literally blocks opioid receptors, making it a kind of forced abstinence drug. Yet the evidence base for Vivitrol, compared to that for methadone and buprenorphine, is weak. It is also far more expensive, at around $1,100 per injection. Nonetheless, naltrexone has received millions of dollars in government funding as well as some heavyweight endorsements. Trump's first health secretary,

Tom Price, stated that though he supported MAT, he disapproved of methadone and buprenorphine because they "simply substitute" one drug for another. Vivitrol lobbyists have also successfully had it added to numerous pieces of state and local legislation at the exclusion of the other two, rather than "letting the market decide."

The expansion of drug courts is another example of the suppression of evidence-based policymaking, as lawmakers say one thing but do another. Drug courts have received millions in government funding during the overdose crisis. On one level, the bipartisan support for this intervention is easy to understand. Drug court advocates pitch the intervention as a way of connecting people to treatment without putting them through the traditional criminal justice system. Yet the reality is not so simple. Admission criteria are so restrictive that many are still forced to face the traditional criminal justice system. Judges are given the authority to make medical decisions outside of their scope of practice. Relapse can be cause for punishment, even though it is a typical component of substance use treatment and recovery. And evidence-based treatments such as buprenorphine and methadone may not be offered to participants—indeed, their use is often penalized.

Even treatment facilities themselves are fraught with systemic issues, including poor integration with traditional medical treatment, a lack of qualified and trained staff, limited implementation of evidence-based practices, and little regulatory oversight. The pharmaceutical deregulation Murch details has occurred alongside the explosion of the "rehab" industry, one of the most unregulated, reckless, and dangerous in health care. It is no surprise to see companies that run private prisons increasingly involved in a lucrative treatment-industrial complex worth $35 billion. It is not simply that these programs are a waste of money; poor-quality health care kills. People who do not get adequate treatment are at high risk of relapse and overdose.

And we must not forget that even if the United States has embraced the rhetoric (rather than reality) of compassion domestically, the same cannot be said for U.S. foreign policy. The United States has exported its drug war to Latin America and beyond, sending weapons and military support to corrupt governments across the world. Billions of dollars are spent and thousands of lives lost in places such as Mexico and Honduras, at the behest of the United States. There is no compassion here, rhetorical or otherwise. Instead we see the truth. The global war on drugs is about imposing U.S. policies and practices on countries with majority black and brown people. In 2006, when Mexico passed a bill decriminalizing possession of small amounts of certain drugs, including cannabis and cocaine, George W. Bush called President Vicente Fox and pushed him to block the bill. Fox obliged and vetoed it.

In short, though U.S. drug policy has tried to present a more compassionate face, it is still rotten at its core. The drug war continues unabated, with drug arrests and incarceration near record highs. It is simply taking on new forms, morphing to keep up with changing winds in public sentiment. The War on Drugs has always been about control—control of communities of color, control of countries, and control of capital, often under the guise of benevolence, paternalism, and compassion. Until we confront these truths, we will never begin to make real change.

The Supremacy of Toughness

Julilly Kohler–Hausmann

AT THE HEART of Donna Murch's analysis is a warning: the drug war is not dead. For Donald Trump, after all, getting tough is the answer to most problems, from trade deficits and violent crime to protesting football players. Even in the midst of an opioid crisis that has been characterized as a "gentler drug war," Trump has explicitly placed toughness at the center of his response. At a speech in New Hampshire in March 2018, for example, he invoked the death penalty as a way to contain the opioid crisis. "We have to get tough on those people," he said. "If we don't get tough on the drug dealers, we're wasting our time."

The president's invocation of a hyper-masculinized vision of political authority is no historical aberration. While Trump takes this performance to a cartoonish extreme (stating, for example, that he would beat Joe Biden in a fist fight), toughness has long shaped—and corrupted—our political discourse, posing the foil of softness as a potentially fatal liability. It was the drive to appear tough on crime that has helped fuel the mass incarceration targeting low-income African American and Latino communities since the 1970s. Legislators and prosecutors engaged in punitive bidding wars, ratcheting up the intensity and duration of punishment for street crime. Many politicians used votes for harsh punishment to showcase their own resolute, muscular political authority or to shield against charges of softness. For decades there appeared to be no upper limit on toughness, despite the fact that harsher sentences were shown to be ineffective deterrents of crime. Throughout the period, the same gendered and racialized logics that privileged prisons and policing were used to defund the welfare state. Opponents of social programs disparaged them as feminine: overly permissive, coddling, and ultimately pathologizing.

It is tempting to conclude that these dynamics have run their course. Activists have transformed mass incarceration into a pressing political problem, in part through laying bare its racist operation and exorbitant costs. Within Democratic Party politics, some politicians are discovering their past support for harsh sentencing to be a liability. In contrast to the draconian state response to crack cocaine, the response to the contemporary opioid crisis is oriented toward treatment.

While these are welcome changes, Murch suggests that celebration would be premature. Compassion is no innovation of the contemporary drug crisis, she shows; it has always been extended along racial lines. White people comprised a minuscule number of those charged with crack-related violations at the federal level, despite making up a majority of the people who used the drug. Conversely, the punitive impulse is hardly absent today. About twenty states now have "drug-induced homicide laws" that allow prosecutors to file murder charges against people who sold drugs that led to an accidental overdose. In 2017 thirteen states considered legislation that would implement or strengthen the ability to charge fatal overdoses as homicides. In many cases, prosecutions targeted an immediate friend or family member that was using drugs with the person who overdosed.

For a half century, almost all participants in drug policy debates have seen a role for both treatment and punishment; they fight over the appropriate balance between them. The struggle is deciding who deserves sympathy, care, and treatment and who requires incarceration, ostracization, quarantine, or death. In sites ranging from courtrooms to hospitals, people tease apart victim from perpetrator or addict from criminal. Yet these categories do not correspond to objective distinctions; the sorting is inevitably contested and subjective. A person's social location —race, ethnicity, neighborhood, gender, and class—has a profound influence over where they fall in the state's taxonomy.

This scheme does not simply shunt users down divergent tracks. It also allocates blame and breeds pernicious social narratives. In the midst of anxiety about suburban drug use in the mid-twentieth century, the visions of a redeemable white drug user depended on the character of the malevolent African American or Latino "pusher" who foisted drugs and addiction onto innocent victims. This is one of many reasons that getting tough remains so effective politically: it identifies easy culprits and sets the terms of debate, helping to sculpt "common sense" about suspect groups by presenting them as manageable only through punishment or physical containment. Trump knows this all too well. His official rhetoric draws an explicit causal link between "illegal aliens" and a whole suite of social ills—"reduced jobs, lower wages, overburdened schools, hospitals that are so crowded you can't get in, increased crime, and a depleted social safety net," as he said in his State of the Union address this year. He also holds them responsible for the "tens of thousands of innocent Americans . . . killed by lethal drugs that cross our border and flood into our cities."

Getting tough exploits a gender hierarchy to naturalize those state strategies, policies, and institutions portrayed as masculine. In this vision of legitimate power, social order is protected by a patriarchal, resolute authority figure at the helm of a resolute, disciplinary state. This logic serves to reproduce a world where men remain the most respected state actors, and traditionally masculinist institutions—the military, police, prisons—are the dominant, most legitimate state tools to manage society. This scheme not only disadvantages the women who hope to gain access to traditionally male-dominated halls of power. It also subordinates state tools that are cast through this gendered rhetoric as "soft," such as cash assistance, social welfare programs, drug treatment, and other branches of the so-called "nanny state."

The supremacy of tough policy and tough politicians impoverishes political discourse. When disputes over drug policy focus on who deserves punishment, the debate is trained on interventions at the level of individuals, obscuring root causes and constricting imagination about alternative futures. Getting tough remains attractive because it is easy; cracking down on drug sellers and undocumented immigrants is simpler than addressing structural inequality and confronting enormously powerful interests, such as the pharmaceutical and health insurance lobbies. To truly transform the dynamics of race, profit, and dispossession that so intensify the harms of drugs, we must subvert the preeminence of macho political authority and resist the impulse to parse out blame at the level of individuals.

Kohler-Hausmann

Denying Racism

Jonathan Kahn

THE WAR ON DRUGS is one of the most ill-conceived, racist, and harmful government initiatives of the past half century. Yet it was also very effective—just not in the way its proponents claimed. The successes have been in politics, not in public health. By all indications, the health challenges presented by drug abuse today are as bad as they have ever been. But over this same period, the Republican Party has effectively reconfigured itself as a party of white racial backlash against the relatively progressive racial and economic policies of the Great Society and the New Deal. From Nixon's Southern Strategy to Reagan's states' rights speech at the Neshoba County Fair and Donald Trump's entire campaign and administration, Republicans have leveraged white racial resentment to shift political narratives and claim power at all levels of government.

Donna Murch convincingly connects Trump's racist ramblings about the opioid crisis and immigration to a much broader field of racialized (and racist) rhetoric and policy that has informed the U.S. government's approach to managing licit and illicit drugs in this country for over a century. But while that history has deep roots in our political institutions and in the capitalist structure of the drug market, it is important to highlight the distinctiveness of the current era.

Murch speaks, for example, of the "paradoxical relationship between a racialized regime of illegal drug prohibition and a highly commercial, laissez-faire approach to prescription pharmaceuticals." There is certainly a relationship here, but why is it "paradoxical"? A racist system's denial of its racism does not render it paradoxical. To the contrary, a denial of racism is wholly consistent with how racism works. It is even, one might say, the predominant rhetorical technique of racism in our supposedly "post-racial" time.

Consider the phenomenon of what might be called "race exhaustion" in U.S. history. By this I mean the common complaint that it is finally time to stop playing the race grievance card. Slavery is long gone; Jim Crow is dead; it is time to move on. This argument has been around as long as there have been post-slavery civil rights laws. In 1883, while striking the Civil Rights Act of 1875, the Supreme Court declared, "When a man has emerged from slavery, and, by the aid of beneficent legislation, has shaken off the inseparable concomitants of that state, there must be some stage in the progress of his elevation when he takes the rank of a mere citizen and ceases to be the special favorite of the laws."

As in 1883, when the passage of a mere eighteen years was deemed sufficient to eradicate the legacy of centuries of slavery, so too in 2013, as Justice John Roberts struck down key portions of the 1965 Voting Rights Act in *Shelby v. Holder* because "things have changed dramatically" since it was enacted. Those resisting racial progress are always pleading some form of race exhaustion and seeking to consign racism to an irrelevant past. It was this attitude that Lyndon Johnson firmly rejected in 1965 in his commencement address at Howard University. "You do not take a person who, for years, has been hobbled by chains and liberate him," he said, "bring him up to the starting line of a race and then say, 'you are free to compete with all the others,' and still justly believe that you have been completely fair." While it is a mistake to view Johnson as some sort of white savior, his forceful distinction between "equality as a right and a theory" and "equality as a fact and equality as a result" helps to explain why the relationship at the heart of Murch's analysis is not paradoxical so much as it is pathological.

Racism endures, then, even as it takes on different forms. And it is not always easy to recognize its manifestations in one's own time. Understanding this is essential to understanding the persisting influence of racism in our society, which Murch masterfully exposes. It is also important to understand that such manifestations are not monolithic. While Murch is right that Democrats are hardly blameless, the contemporary racism she identifies has a distinctively Republican provenance. After all, the liberals on the Supreme Court vigorously dissented in *Shelby v. Holder*, and it has largely been Democratic governors and attorneys general who have been filing lawsuits against the Trump administration to challenge such racist actions as the Muslim Ban and declaring a national emergency to fund the border wall.

In parsing the broad concept of racial capitalism in relation to U.S. law and policy, it is useful to consider Murch's analysis alongside the work of legal scholars Nancy Leong and Cheryl Harris. Leong defines racial capitalism more particularly as "the process of deriving social and economic value from the racial identity of another person." She is especially interested in the way "white individuals and predominantly white institutions use nonwhite people to acquire social and economic value" in the context of programs such as affirmative action and diversity hiring, which recognize marginalized identities as desirable in order to reap both material and symbolic dividends. Harris provides a complementary frame in her essay "Whiteness as Property," which reaches back to the 1896 case of *Plessy v. Ferguson* to examine the ways whiteness has literally been capitalized to provide value in forms ranging from reputation to real estate. Part of Homer Plessy's original suit involved a claim that, because he was an "octoroon"—one-eighth black—forcing him to sit in a blacks-only car deprived him of the reputational value accorded by the seven-eighths of him that was white. Few realize today that during the early twentieth century many states recognized a tort of racial defamation, whereby a white plaintiff could claim injury for being improperly called black.

All of this is to say that racial capitalism involves more than a capitalistic system built on racial oppression. It has taken on distinct and particular forms in different eras. The forms identified by Leong and Harris contrast with the prevailing politics of Trump's new Republican party. Unlike Leong's racial capitalism of affirmative action (which exploits people of color as symbolic goods) and Harris's notion of whiteness as property (which exploits the positive value of white racial identity), the racial capitalism of Trump's War on Drugs is negative, exploiting communities of color as scapegoats and foils. It invokes tropes of Mexican invaders as a means to distract from the sins of Big Pharma in facilitating the opioid crisis. Race thus takes on a new kind of capital value: scapegoating Mexicans protects pharma's capital by cleansing it of responsibility. And this new racialized scapegoat is made to bear not only the burden of imputed sin, but also the burden of government surveillance, oversight, and incarceration. The "value" of racism here lies not in extracting labor from subordinated bodies, and not solely—as Murch shows in the case of racialized prescription drugs—in creating addicted consumers and capturing racial markets. It also lies in diversion.

Of course, scapegoating is an ancient practice. And specifically racial scapegoating in the United States has a long and sordid past, most clearly evident today in the lynchings commemorated by the solemn steel rectangles hanging from the ceiling of the National Memorial for Peace and Justice in Montgomery. Purdue Pharma has scapegoated its victims by trying to blame them for their addiction. In this context, what makes the old new again is Trump's explicit appeal to race, not simply in the service of white supremacy, but additionally and directly in the service of corporate supremacy. Here, perhaps, is where we see racism and capitalism most completely intertwined in this story.

From Absolution to Accountability

L.A. Kauffman

FROM OUR VANTAGE POINT, lying on the floor, watching the protest unfold was almost hypnotic. Thousands of white paper slips—representing OxyContin scripts—floated slowly down through the grand white atrium of the Guggenheim Museum, while a small group of us stretched out on the ground, representing a tiny fraction of those who have died from the drug.

To my right lay Nan Goldin, the celebrated artist who launched our activist group, Prescription Addiction Intervention Now (P.A.I.N.), after struggling with opioid addiction for years and nearly losing her life to an overdose. Next to her was Robert Suarez, a leading harm reduction advocate with the group Voices of Community Activists and Leaders (VOCAL-NY), whose mother died in his arms as a consequence of her opioid dependency. White-coated medical students from New York University lay off to the side, along with people living in recovery from substance-use disorders. Above us, holding bright red banners along the white spiral ramps of the Frank Lloyd Wright building, were others who have experienced the crisis up close: a group of mothers whose children died from overdose, friends and family of people struggling with addiction, organizers who have been fighting to establish the country's first legal safe injection facilities.

We had taken over the museum to demand that it refuse future funding from the Sackler family, the pharmaceutical clan that has made billions in profit from OxyContin sales, and remove signs that honor their name. The mock prescriptions alluded to the recent disclosure of Richard Sackler's chilling 1996 boast that "the launch of OxyContin tablets will be followed by a blizzard of prescriptions that will bury the competition." Our banners captured our message succinctly: "400,000 DEAD," read one, summarizing the staggering losses caused by the family's ghoulish path to wealth. "TAKE DOWN THEIR NAME."

Donna Murch writes powerfully of the "space of white absolution that enabled the profitable mass-marketing of licit pharmaceuticals" in recent decades, even as black and brown Americans were being incarcerated en masse for selling or using substances whose difference from prescription medicines "has more to do with race, class, and differential application of state power than pharmacology."

For our group, on that evening this past February, that "space of white absolution" was no metaphor. The Guggenheim is one of many museums that have quite literally provided space for the Sackler family to whitewash their many misdeeds and cast themselves as beneficent figures despite their direct role in destroying so many lives. Just beneath the floor where we held our die-in is the Sackler Center for Arts Education, one of many prestigious facilities named after the family.

A year into her recovery, Goldin published a collection of photographs in *Artforum* that juxtaposed her own experience of OxyContin addiction with the laudatory Sackler signage that graces so many eminent institutions, from the monumental Sackler Wing at New York's Metropolitan Museum to the porcelain-tiled Sackler Courtyard at the Victoria and Albert Museum in London. "They have washed their blood money through the halls of museums and universities around the world," she wrote. Our protest at the Guggenheim was our fourth major museum disruption to hold the Sackler family accountable, after similar actions at the Met, the Smithsonian, and the Harvard Art Museums.

As we undertook these actions, we privately heard many objections from museum officials: that cultural institutions are starved for adequate funding, that all great fortunes derive from unsavory sources, that museums would go bankrupt if they were required to vet every gift to meet the moral standards of the day. The naming agreements, we have been told, were made in perpetuity and are set in stone. Our actions came as numerous museums are facing protest and public critique for ties to controversial benefactors. Among them are the Whitney Museum, whose vice chairman, Warren Kanders, owns the tear-gas manufacturer Safariland, described by scholar Anna Feigenbaum as a "one-stop shop" for protest repression, and the Metropolitan Museum, whose billionaire patron David H. Koch is a leading climate-change accelerator and denier.

The history of philanthropy is of course a history of burnishing the reputations of the very rich, giving a high-culture gloss to tawdry accumulation and conferring social capital on those with financial capital. "Think of it, ye millionaires of many markets," an original trustee of the Met, Joseph Choate, famously declared in 1880, "what glory may yet be yours, if you only listen to our advice, to convert pork into porcelain, grain and produce into priceless pottery, the rude ores of commerce into sculptured marble." In the case of the Sacklers, though, it was not pork that was converted first into profit and then into porcelain, but human autonomy, dignity, and life, on an almost unfathomable scale. The way that this family has for so long escaped any real consequences for their direct role in hundreds of thousands of deaths—even as hundreds of thousands of Americans, disproportionately black and brown, are caged behind bars for nonviolent drug-related offenses—epitomizes the divisions and paradoxes that Murch explores. The racialized logic of the War on Drugs and the opioid crisis has produced outlandish punishment for some, outlandish indemnity for others.

This is the larger context in which the Sacklers managed, until very recently, to evade legal prosecution for their actions and still find their name honored by some of the world's most eminent cultural institutions, despite deliberately deceiving doctors about the strength and addictive potential of their profitable drug. The family's cynical path to prestige embodies a larger and very toxic culture of impunity in our time that has gone hand in hand with growing concentrations of wealth and power. As the extreme inequality of this era takes ever more oligarchic and authoritarian forms, the carte blanche long given to the Sacklers calls to mind the ways that Donald Trump has escaped consequences for boasting of sexual assault or calling neo-Nazis "very fine people." This is a time of craven capitulation to bad-acting billionaires, and the fact that leading arts institutions took steps to distance themselves from the Sacklers only after they faced high-profile protest recalls the gutless way so many political figures have normalized the presidency of a man who lied to the public more than 8,000 times in his first 2 years in office. The story of the Sacklers exemplifies a pervasive pattern of exoneration for those at the top of economic, racial, and gendered hierarchies, which the #BlackLivesMatter and #MeToo movements have both worked to highlight and challenge.

From an organizer's point of view, the processes of racial capitalism that Murch outlines are so massive that they can be difficult to address head-on. But it is precisely because systems of power reinforce each other in complex and nuanced ways that an oblique approach can at times have broad impact. It is because there are cultural logics to these systems that challenges on cultural and symbolic fronts can spark wider change. The fight to take down the Sackler name is similar, in this regard, to campaigns by anti-racist organizers to take down Confederate monuments: removing these symbols does not correct the evils they celebrate, but allowing them to stand is so culturally corrosive that it impedes any fuller reckoning.

In itself, halting Sackler funding and removing the Sackler name from cultural institutions will not expropriate the family's wealth and reallocate it to treatment and harm reduction or lead to any direct legal consequences. On its own, it certainly will not begin to solve the opioid crisis or address the deeper structures of racial capitalism that have allowed Big Pharma to profit so mightily and blamelessly from mass addiction. Even as P.A.I.N. has focused most strongly on seeking change from museums and cultural institutions, we have worked closely with groups promoting other transformative solutions: helping VOCAL-NY set up a mock safe injection site right on the busy avenue in front of New York governor Andrew Cuomo's Manhattan office as part of a campaign to seek approval for these lifesaving interventions, and supporting the introduction of the CARE Act, a measure that would allocate billions to those on the frontlines of the opioid crisis to implement compassionate treatment on a massive scale.

As we lay there on the ground floor of the Guggenheim during our disruption, we were extending a larger invitation: to imagine what might happen if the spaces of white absolution were transformed into spaces of accountability, if cultural institutions showed the courage to stand up for the human values they ostensibly champion. We had no way of knowing that within six weeks of our protest, the Guggenheim would refuse all future gifts from the Sacklers, following close on the heels of similar moves by the National Portrait Gallery in London and the Tate museums. Or that eight members of the family would—for the first time—be personally sued in a massive legal action by hundreds of cities, counties, and Native American tribes. Or that the Sacklers would suspend all of their philanthropy in the United Kingdom. We cannot and do not take credit for all these developments; whatever impact our direct actions had, they channeled and amplified the already existing outrage of millions and built on much brilliant work by journalists, advocates, and attorneys. But accountability, we learned, can have its own momentum, with culture as the catalyst.

Public Policy Made Americans the Biggest Consumers of Opioids in the World

Donna Murch

RACIAL CAPITALISM, this forum has shown, is a powerful analytical tool. It provides a framework robust enough to account for the racial logic of the opioid crisis, the Trump-era War on Drugs, and the country's punitive turn. The responses to my essay expand its reach even further, offering multiple points of departure for enriching the narrative. Our conversation highlights the power of integrating public health scholarship and activism with writings on mass incarceration and the drug war. It was not until I attempted to suture together different threads of this story, drawing on both schools of thought, that I saw how much the narrative arc of drug prohibition changes in light of the recent history of Big Pharma.

The core paradox of the opioid crisis is how extreme criminalization of a racialized, illicit drug economy underwrote and enabled the larger project of licit drug deregulation. The United States is simultaneously the largest incarcerator of people convicted of using and selling drugs *and* the largest consumer of legal (and illegal) narcotics in the developed world, by far. Although Americans make up only 5 percent of the world's population, they consume over 80 percent of the world's opioids. Public policy has enabled the steady growth of pharmaceutical consumption as multiple iterations of the drug war raged on. And of course, as in all aspects of U.S. society, race functions as the structuring principle, in this case dividing the aboveground and netherworld of drug business. As Britt Rusert notes in her response, "We continue to live in a world made by Reagan, one where corporate empowerment both benefits from and reinforces racial regimes of punishment."

Not content to limit our analysis of racial capitalism to the contemporary United States, Max Mishler demonstrates that the creative destruction of family-owned drug "cartels" is far from new. Drawing explicitly on black Marxist thinker Eric Williams and implicitly on Alfred McCoy's *The Politics of Heroin in Southeast Asia* (1972), Mishler offers a compelling counter-history that places the opioid crisis in a *longue durée* history of imperialism. He emphasizes the protean and flexible nature of racial capitalism, which "bracketed" white drug addiction while escalating "concern about racialized laboring populations" in the United States. Emphasizing the links between expanding markets, imperial violence, and psychoactive substances—whether opium, alcohol, tobacco, cocaine, or sugar—remains a uniquely compelling way to teach the global history of racial capitalism. One of the truisms of U.S. drug histories is that every major foreign war of the past century produced a domestic drug crisis. Mishler's analysis helps to explain why.

Although the historiography is slowly expanding, racial capitalism has not found wide currency among carceral historians until quite recently with the exciting new work of LaShawn Harris, Max Felker-Kantor, Jackie Wang, and Simon Balto, among others. Geographer Ruth Wilson Gilmore's pathbreaking Marxist analysis *Golden Gulag* (2007) is an important influence, exploring surplus land, labor, and capital as the driving forces behind California's postwar prison boom.

Nevertheless, in contrast to the public's fascination with private prisons, many historians view hyper-incarceration as a political project at its core. While certain aspects of the contemporary carceral state can be parsed as revenue-generating state action—including bail, immigrant detention, Ferguson-style municipal fines and fees, and civil asset forfeiture—the carceral project is an expensive one whose primary yield has been greater control over nonwhite populations and accrual of political capital in the years after the 1965 Voting Rights Act. Investigative journalist Dan Baum's notorious interview with John Erhlichman succinctly encapsulates this view. "The Nixon campaign in 1968, and the Nixon White House after that, had two enemies: the antiwar left and black people," explained the Watergate coconspirator in 1994. "We knew we couldn't make it illegal to be either against the war or black, but by getting the public to associate the hippies with marijuana and blacks with heroin, and then criminalizing both heavily, we could disrupt those communities. We could arrest their leaders, raid their homes, break up their meetings, and vilify them night after night on the evening news. Did we know we were lying about the drugs? Of course we did."

This is an issue not only of the past, but of the eternal present. On the eve of Jair Bolsonaro's election in Brazil this past October and Trump's multiple meetings with Philippine president Rodrigo Duterte, the punitive language of the drug war has once again been deployed in service of right-wing authoritarianism. As Dawn Paley's work on "drug war capitalism" clearly demonstrates, the Wars on Drugs and Gangs are protean abstractions that never reduced consumption of illicit substances. They did, however, enable a portfolio of revanchist policies around the globe—from police killings in Brazilian favelas to land grabs in Colombia, summary executions in the Philippines and the warehousing and economic divestment of vulnerable populations throughout the West. To explain how this happened, Michael Collins reminds us that the United States globalized the War on Drugs by "imposing U.S. policies and practices" throughout the developing world.

Bringing our attention back to the domestic sphere, Julilly Kohler-Hausmann highlights how the drug war spawned a governing rationale not only for the Trump administration, but also for his Democratic and Republican predecessors. From the 1970s forward, "getting tough" became the "answer to most problems," from disciplining poor women on state assistance to trade deficits. Kohler argues that at its core, the War on Drugs and its predilection for toughness hinged on a "gender hierarchy" privileging traditionally masculinist institutions of the state, including police, military, and prisons. This analysis is critical, and Kohler-Hausmann's work on Nelson Rockefeller's "Attila the Hun laws" demonstrates the urgency of integrating racial and gender analysis to understand the punitive turn.

Jonathan Kahn, by contrast, sees the Trump presidency and drug war as the culmination of Republican dominance in the recent past. As a result, the tension between drug deregulation of legal markets and the criminalization of illicit trade is understood not as paradox, but as GOP racial scapegoating. However, this premise contradicts much of what we know about the War on Crime, which scholars Naomi Murakawa and Elizabeth Hinton have revealed as a bipartisan project from its very inception in President Lyndon Johnson's administration. Here it is useful to recall one of the most absurd moments in the Trump presidency, when he threatened in a speech before the United Nations to introduce legislation sentencing drug dealers to death. In his rush to "get tough," Trump remained blissfully unaware that the powers to do so at the federal level had already been granted by Democratic president Bill Clinton in his 1994 crime bill. This irony highlights why we need a searching moral inventory of the overlapping Wars on Drugs, Gangs, and Crime that is critical of the Trump presidency's virulent racism, but does not see it as exceptional. Trump's administration cannot be understood apart from a deeper history of how the two-party system nurtured the racial animus of mass incarceration across party lines.

Understanding our history is nowhere more urgent than in the upcoming primary race for the 2020 presidential election. Thanks to Black Lives Matter and other radical activists, the last presidential election saw a robust critique of the Clintons' participation in the incarceration frenzy. That same critique has now been trained on Kamala Harris's record as California's attorney general. But it is crucial that we also openly debate Joe Biden's pivotal role in mass incarceration and the drug war. Many today see him as an heir to Barack Obama, but he bragged in the 1990s that, in hindsight, the Republican Party resembled Abbie Hoffman and the Democratic Party J. Edgar Hoover in matters of tough crime control. To this end, Biden fought tirelessly for expansion of the death penalty and increased mandatory minimums and civil forfeiture. He helped create the kinds of policies that Trump, Jeff Sessions, and William Barr have so cynically used to their advantage. Just as we hold Harris accountable for her comments on incarcerating the parents of truants, so too should we scrutinize Biden and other Democrats' culpability in mass criminalization.

It is impossible to write about the opioid crisis and the War on Drugs without looking forward to solutions. Michael Collins's emphasis on moving away from unregulated, pharmaceutical-driven drug treatment and failed criminal justice reform policies such as drug courts points toward new types of activism. Similarly, L.A. Kauffman's beautifully written firsthand account of P.A.I.N's Guggenheim protest against the Sacklers' patronage reminds us that collective action is our most powerful tool for dismantling our prison nation *and* for holding corporations such as Purdue Pharma accountable.

Finally, Helena Hansen, Julie Netherland, and David Herzberg, whose transformative work helped inspire my essay, chart the opioid epidemic's change over time. As is clearly evident in New York, overdose rates among African Americans are rising precipitously, and a singular focus on white suffering occludes the full range of public health effects. Equally important is their analysis of buprenorphine and other forms of medication-assisted treatment (MAT). They demonstrate how pharmaceutical regimes of racial capitalism shape *both* drug use and treatment, thereby deepening underlying race and class disparities. For this reason, technological fixes rooted in the same industry that spawned the opioid crisis will never provide the antidote. Only a broad-based, anti-racist campaign that diverts resources from punishment and corporate subsidy to public health can move us, in the words of Kauffman, from absolution to accountability.

Bankers and Empire

Peter James Hudson

SCRUBBED FROM THE PAGES of glossy coffee-table books, the history of U.S. imperialism can be found in the archives of Wall Street's oldest, largest, and most powerful institutions. A deep dive into the vaults and ledgers of banking houses such as Citigroup, Inc., and J. P. Morgan Chase and Co. reveals a story of capitalism and empire whose narrative is not of morally pure and inspiring economic growth, technological innovation, market expansion, and shareholder accumulation, but rather of blood and labor, stolen sovereignty and pilfered resources, military occupation and monetary control. Sugar comingles with blood, chain gangs cross spur lines, and the magical abstractions of finance are found vulgarized in the base manifestations of racial capitalism.

This history of bankers and empire is also a Caribbean history. The Caribbean archipelago was ground zero for U.S. imperial banking.

Wall Street's first experiments in internationalism occurred in Cuba, Haiti, Panama, Puerto Rico, the Dominican Republic, and Nicaragua, often with disastrous results—for those countries and colonies, and often for the imperial banks themselves. Yet where there was expansion, there was also pushback. The internationalization of Wall Street was met with local resistance, refusal and revolt. And just as the history of imperialism has been excised from popular narratives, so too has this history of Caribbean anti-imperialism and autonomy.

THE HISTORY OF imperial banking and racial capitalism begins at the end of the nineteenth century, at the historical horizon where the project of U.S. settler colonialism that spurred the financing of the West became the enterprise of U.S. territorial colonialism in the Caribbean and Asia.

Buoyed by unprecedented wealth and boosted by the expansionist jingoism following the victory over Spain in the Caribbean and the Pacific, New York City's bankers and merchants believed that the organization of an imperial banking system—one that could compete with Europe's long-established institutions—was critical to the global rise of the city and to the consolidation of Wall Street's position in international finance, trade, and commerce. With these ambitions, bankers and business-people set their sights on asserting control over the trade and finance of the Americas. They sought to control local central banks, establish U.S. branch banks, take over commodity financing, reorganize monetary systems on a dollar basis, and refinance European-funded sovereign debt.

This project of internationalization was explicitly encouraged and supported by the U.S. government. The war and state departments required fiscal agencies to support the infrastructure of U.S. colonialism, and financial institutions were an important conduit of colonial policy and financial and commercial diplomacy. Bankers, however, needed little prodding to move overseas, extending their influence into the sugar plantations, railroads, and financial systems of Haiti, Cuba, Santo Domingo, and Nicaragua. The U.S. state made both implicit and explicit assurances that it would intervene should local conditions turn against U.S. business interests or disrupt the payments of interest or customs revenue.

At the center of this story was the National City Bank of New York, the precursor to today's Citigroup, Inc. Founded in 1812, it emerged as the largest and most important imperial financier in the United States. Through most of the nineteenth century, it was a powerful but staid merchant bank whose cautious lending and massive cash reserves helped it ride the nation's economic roils. It took on a more aggressive, entrepreneurial, and activist strategy for expansion and growth under James Stillman and Frank A. Vanderlip, who carried it into the twentieth century.

Stillman and Vanderlip transformed City Bank from a merchant bank into a modern financial department store—creating a new managerial structure, expanding into new financial markets, and exploring the possibilities of foreign expansion and international banking. The most important theater of internationalization was the "American Mediterranean," as one City Banker described the countries and colonies ringing the Caribbean Sea and the Gulf of Mexico. There, the bank experimented with the issuance of sovereign debt, the financing of international trade, the funding of industrial infrastructure, and the organization of regional state banks and currency systems. Beginning in 1914, it also made the Caribbean the centerpiece of the largest foreign branch bank system of any U.S. banking house, with Cuba the jewel in its crown.

Law was critical to City Bank's internationalization and expansion. As part of its efforts, City Bank hammered away at the banking regulations shackling its activities and pushed for regulatory reform while creating new subsidiary organizations that could navigate the complex regulatory geographies of international finance or simply evade existing legal constraint. Wall Street lawyer John Sterling, of Shearman and Sterling, worked closely with Stillman and Vanderlip, while other firms worked to devise the colonial methods by which the imperial banks operated.

Race was central to City Bank's work, too. In its encounters with the nations and colonies of the Caribbean and Latin America, Wall Street helped reorder those economies along racial lines, exporting the U.S. racist imaginaries in which Wall Street was embedded and through which it functioned. When conducting business in the Caribbean, U.S. bankers understood people of color—whether Africans or indigenous peoples—through the same racist lenses they viewed them through at home. White representations of African Americans, in particular, were exported to the West Indies and inscribed in a vast and diffuse archive of pamphlets, reports, circulars, press releases, prospectuses, and journal articles produced by Wall Street about the Caribbean and Latin America. At the same time, in their dispatches back to the United States, bankers translated the Caribbean to U.S. businesspeople, investors, and the general public. In some cases they debunked stereotypes as a means to encourage investment. In others they replicated and reconstituted racial stereotypes in order to further the expansion of white supremacist control of the region—with returns to investment found not in the extraction of capital values, but in the ledger of white racial dominance.

One example of this practice can be found in City Bank vice president John H. Allen, one of the new slate of managers and vice presidents appointed by Vanderlip as part of the bank's modernization of its bureaucracy. Allen aided the bank's expansion into Cuba and Argentina and was the manager of the City Bank–controlled Banque Nationale de la République d'Haiti in the 1910s. In the City Bank's foreign trade journal *The Americas*, Allen evoked a picture of Haiti that would have been recognizable to white U.S. audiences but for its tropical setting. "Cock-fighting and card playing," Allen asserted, "are the national pastimes, and these, together with a supply of Haitian rum, are all that is necessary for a Haitian citizen's perfect day." He claimed that during his visits to Haiti, he found that "humorous incidents were of almost daily occurrences." For Allen, such incidents "showed the naivete and also the restricted mentality of the people, which latter was plainly noticeable even among the more highly educated."

These anecdotes did not exist in a vacuum. They were not an incidental cultural membrane stretched over the inner workings of banking, racial capitalism, and imperialism. Instead they contributed to the fundamental ideological and cultural rationales that made the Caribbean the target of Wall Street's imperial aims, and at the same time helped fashion the terms through which the Caribbean was encountered. These representations were underwritten by both direct and indirect forms of violence: by coercive diplomacy, military force, and labor impressment, as well as by the terms and conditions of credit and debt, the imbalanced application of law and legal regulation, and the imposition of modern forms of post-emancipation financial governance.

Indeed, Allen himself was deeply involved with the decision to send U.S. Marines to Haiti in 1915 in what would become a nineteen-year military occupation. City Bank had been interested in Haitian investments since about 1910, and Vanderlip sought to use some initial railway and dock investments as a springboard to control the republic's financial system. Haiti's internal political conflicts, fueled in part by outside agitation and interference from both U.S. and European speculators, created disastrous terms for business. In response, City Bank's Roger L. Farnham, who viewed the Haitian people as "nothing but grown-up children" who required the paternalistic guidance of a stronger power, drafted a document arguing for U.S. military intervention to stabilize the country and protect U.S. financial and commercial interests.

The Farnham plan, as it was dubbed, was realized in 1915, when Marines landed to restore order following the assassination of Haitian president Vilbrun Guillaume Sam. The occupation provided the platform for City Bank's takeover of the Banque Nationale while making City Bank's imposition of a $30 million loan to the Haitian government almost risk free. Vanderlip described Haiti as "a small but profitable piece of business" for City Bank. But such profits came at a cost: the suppression of a series of peasant insurgencies that left thousands of Haitians dead and dozens of villages burned. Hundreds of Haitians were jailed or forced to work on chain gangs, serving as a reminder to many Haitians of the days of slavery.

CITY BANK was not the only U.S. financial institution charting an imperial turn. It was joined by its neighbors on Wall Street, sometimes as collaborators involved in a collective project to consolidate the financial realms of the U.S. imperium, sometimes as rivals embroiled in bitter competition.

Chase Manhattan Bank, for instance, made an aggressive push to displace City Bank in Panama while fighting City Bank for pride of place in the financing of the dictatorship of Gerardo Machado y Morales in Cuba. Meanwhile, Wall Street's unincorporated and private investment banks, including J. P. Morgan and Co., Speyer and Co., and Kuhn, Loeb and Co., began floating the public debt of Caribbean, Latin American, and Asian countries, states, and municipalities and financing railroad and port projects. These private bankers had initially grown in prominence by using their strong European networks and their close family ties as the conduit to market U.S. government bonds and corporate securities across the Atlantic. Now, increasingly, they sold Caribbean and Latin American debt in the United States.

Private bankers came to play an important role in the policy of "dollar diplomacy" initiated by President William Howard Taft and his secretary of state, Philander Knox, in the 1910s. In the attempt to displace European influence and extend U.S. capitalism in the Caribbean— which purported to replace military intervention with financial diplomacy—private bankers worked with financial experts and local governments to refund sovereign debt, reorganize customs collection and currency systems, and organize nominally national government banks. The disordered global financial and economic conditions unleashed by World War I accelerated the internationalization of Wall Street and intensified the relationship between banking, bankers, and imperialism.

But the expansion, and this initial experiment in imperial banking, was short lived. The sharp economic crisis following the postwar commodity boom forced a brief retreat from internationalization, prompting many Wall Street institutions, including City Bank, to rethink their strategies for expansion. Meanwhile the local banking sector in Cuba was completely destroyed. Of course, by the end of the 1920s, another crisis had occurred; the concussions of the October 1929 stock market crash were felt not only domestically, but throughout the international branch and subsidiary networks of Wall Street—perhaps most acutely in the Caribbean.

The domestic crisis of finance capitalism in the United States became a crisis of racial capitalism in the Caribbean. As Wall Street's financial edifice imploded, so too did the racial bolsters on which it was constructed. A wave of anti-imperialist and anti–Wall Street sentiment rose across the Caribbean, manifested in the withdrawal of funds from foreign banks, editorials in local newspapers attacking the monopoly presence, worker takeover of foreign-controlled sugar mills, bombings of bank buildings, calls for the nationalization or indigenization of foreign-owned banks, and, in the case of Cuba, calls for the renunciation of foreign debt.

These assertions of sovereignty were not only a claim for economic independence; they were also a rejection of the governing tropes of racial paternalism. Moreover, the rejection of finance capitalism and imperial banking served as a rejection of white supremacy and the obliteration of the circular logic associating whites with wealth and wealth with whites. The desire to break the hold and allure of City Bank and other U.S. banking and investment firms meant a challenge to the divine laws of racial capitalism. In these calls for the nationalization or indigenization of state banking, and in the cries to default on sovereign debt, was a refusal to be governed through the implicitly hierarchal—and implicitly racialized—international orders that had subordinated these countries to the United States.

It was also an effort to critique the registers of profitmaking and accumulation through which the Caribbean labor that produced products —especially sugar—was obscured, shrouded, and hidden in the commodity form itself. The radical journalist Carleton Beals captured this process in *The Crime of Cuba* (1933), his account of U.S. finance capital —of Chase Bank and City Bank—and the Machado dictatorship. Early in the book, in his discussion of the racialized political economy of sugar, Beals evokes Karl Marx's description of the commodity as a "social hieroglyphic" whose meaning is only revealed through exegetical means. "For most Americans, Cuba is but the hieroglyphic of a ticker," Beals writes: "Amer. Sugar 26 5/8 / Cub. Amer. Sugar 17 1/7 / Cub. Am. Pfd. 18 1/5." He goes further, unpacking, or deciphering, the meaning of sugar as the story of the capture of black labor power. "But for me," Beals writes, "all this inner mystery is forever imprisoned in each cube of white sugar I drop into my morning coffee. Black Cuba and black sweat and black song and dance, crystallized into a snow cube, held in silver prongs."

Often such critiques occurred under the guises of the Communist Party and the Comintern, especially through their efforts to build a global movement of radical black labor. The literature and propaganda of black communists at this time linked racial, or what was called "national," oppression of black workers to finance capital and imperialism. The pages of the *Negro Worker*, for instance, contained denunciations of City Bank's involvement in Haiti alongside accounts of black labor exploitation and colonial oppression across the African diaspora. The magazine was published under the auspices of the International Trade Union's Committee of Negro Workers, a branch of the Red International Labour Union and an appendage of the Comintern tasked with mobilizing black labor in worldwide class struggle against global capitalism.

The paper's one-time editor George Padmore also cataloged global conditions of black exploitation in his *Life and Struggles of Negro Toilers*, published in 1931. Padmore was a young black Trinidadian functionary for the Communist Party's Negro wing and a prolific writer. *Life and Struggles of Negro Toilers* presents a sweeping comparative account of the conditions suffered by black people in Africa and the African diaspora and includes attacks on early twentieth-century U.S. expansionism overseas and, with it, the transformation of Haiti and the Dominican Republic, and Liberia and Abyssinia, into colonies of U.S. finance capital. Padmore assails City Bank's imposition of debt on the Dominican Republic and the transformation of Haiti into "an American slave colony" during the U.S. occupation. He lambasts the "'Black Ivory' Trade"—the conscription of Haitian workers to the Cuban plantations of the General Sugar Company and the United Fruit Company. He argues that Haitians were brought to the country "in the same ways as chattel slaves of former days." Haitians were underpaid, indebted to their contractors, and housed in segregated and unsanitary barracoons. In Padmore's writing, finance capitalism was racial capitalism.

Similar critiques were implicit in Jacques Roumain's novel *Masters of the Dew* (1941). The founder of the Haitian Communist Party, Roumain was jailed during the waning days of the U.S. occupation. *Masters of the Dew* centers on a Haitian *bracero* who returns to his country from Cuba and attempts to rebuild Haiti through collective labor and a call for black autonomy. For Roumain, the collective pull of the *coumbite* (farmers' cooperative) replaces the coercive push of the *corvée* (forced-labor gang).

At the same time, U.S. banking and corporate interests became the subject of a radical, anti-imperialist Caribbean literature—a literature that can be viewed as a counterpoint to the rhetoric of City Bank and attempts by Wall Street to "visualize" the Caribbean, to borrow Allen's term, for the purposes of exploitation and accumulation. Cuban poet Nicolás Guillén's *West Indies, Ltd.* (1934), for instance, satirically attacks the corporate transformation of the Caribbean into "the grotesque headquarters of companies and trusts." In Nicaraguan novelist's Hernán Robleto's *Los estrangulados* (1933), the Brown Brothers and J. W. Seligman–controlled Banco Nacional de Nicaragua and the Mercantile Bank of the Americas' Compañía Mercantil de Ultramar feature as dominant and domineering institutions undermining the economic independence of the Nicaraguan elite through its loaning practices. Langston Hughes wrote of the role of City Bank not only in Haiti but also in Cuba. He evokes the transitions from mercantilism to imperialism and colonialism to neocolonialism in Cuba's history and offers a glum assessment of the ability of "the Little Fort of San Lazaro," standing sentinel at the entrance to Havana's harbor, facing the Caribbean Sea and the United States, to repel the pillaging of finance capitalism. "But now," writes Hughes, "Against a pirate called / THE NATIONAL CITY BANK / What can you do alone?"

Hudson

Pushback against racial capitalism did not occur only under the auspices of the Communist Party. Caribbean intellectuals also turned inward to seek out an autochthonous, anti-imperial critique that was the precursor to the philosophy of Négritude. This phenomenon was perhaps most pronounced in Haiti. For the Haitian elite, the utter humiliation of the U.S. occupation forced them to rethink their identities. Their longstanding identifications with France and European Enlightenment thought and culture proved an absurdity in the face of the brutal racism of the U.S. occupation. Many among them realized they were suffering from what Jean Price-Mars called a "collective bovarism"—a deluded and misrecognized sense of self. The Haitian elite slowly realized that Europe was not their home. Africa was. Price-Mars's *Ainsi Parla l'Oncle*, an ethnological exploration of the culture and folklore of the Haitian peasantry and its African origins, published in Port-au-Prince in 1927, helped spur the development of insurgent literary and national cultures in the Caribbean and throughout the African diaspora.

In Cuba, this turn to blackness as an alternative to racial capitalism took on multiple and contradictory forms. In the early 1920s, writers such as Jesús Masdeu, in *La raza triste* (1924), depicted the black workers in the Cuban sugar mills in sentimental, romantic, and often paternal tones. The racial paternalism began to slip away in *La danza de los millones* (1923), Venezuelan expatriate Rafael Antonio Cisneros's experimental novel with its efforts at narrating the effects of the banking crisis of 1920–21 on his black characters. In *La zafra* (1926), a collection of "combat poems," Cuba's Agustín Acosta recounted the effects of the sugar boom and bust on the country, linking finance capital to racial capitalism, and sugar to blackness, money, and the poison of U.S. empire. Acosta made this explicit in the poem "La danza de los millones." It evokes the incursion of the instruments and techniques of U.S. finance capital into the Cuban economy, portraying it as a turbulent sea threatening to capsize the ship of Cuba's sovereignty. Acosta warned of "Wall Street, with its usurious bankers." In the novel *¡Écue-Yamba-Ó!* written by a young Alejo Carpentier while in Machado's prison in 1927, blackness was rendered as the soul of Cuban culture, and an African alterity became the terms of a critique of imperialism and white finance. "El bongo," Carpentier wrote, "Antídoto de Wall Street!"

THE ANTIDOTE TO Wall Street did not prove to be a cure. Certainly, changes occurred and the crises of the 1930s forced Wall Street to rethink the organization of finance capital and the project of internationalization in a new era of governance, regulation, and sovereignty. In Haiti, City Bank sold the Banque Nationale to the Haitian government but kept its management structure and its ties to Wall Street in place. In the Dominican Republic, City Bank's branches became the basis for a national banking system, but U.S. capital still dominated the country. In Cuba, attempts to renounce Chase Bank's debts and default on amortization payments were stalled by the Cuban courts, and it would take another three decades before Wall Street was finally expelled from the country.

Meanwhile, City Bank and Chase Bank would spend the next decades struggling to return to the heady days of unregulated expansion and unbounded freedom that characterized the early twentieth-century history of imperial banking, writing anew the Caribbean ledger of finance and racial capitalism.

Branded

Jordanna Matlon

IN THE PHOTOGRAPH *Branded Head* (2003), the shape of a black man's clean-shaven head gracefully curves against a plain white background. The subject's face—and with it all the features that might have identified him—is outside of the frame. The viewer's attention is drawn instead to a keloid several inches above his ear in the shape of the Nike swoosh. The man is branded.

The portrait is a searing critique of what its creator, artist Hank Willis Thomas, calls a *commodifiable* blackness. "Young African American men especially," Thomas observes, "have been known to pay to become the best advertisers anyone could ask for." Without the Nike swoosh, Thomas's subject would be entirely anonymous, a faceless black body. Branded, he becomes recognizable—yet in a way that accepts commodification as the source of his identity.

For Thomas, *Branded Head* speaks to how little has changed across the different eras of racial capitalism. "Slaves," he explains, "were branded as a sign of ownership and . . . today so many of us brand ourselves." In the first instance, branding was a mark of lost agency, a conversion of the body into a commodity object. Now branding—commodification—ironically restores value, in a postindustrial era that so often construes the black body as lacking any intrinsic value.

It is undeniable that our culture's obsession with branding cuts across race and gender. Nonetheless there is something unique about how black men participate in it, and that speaks to their location within the structure of racial capitalism. For much of capitalism's history, after all, its protagonists—the property owners and wage laborers who, as Marx would say, were destined to "make history"—were all white men. This legacy of entitlement persists in the inequalities we see today, which so often render *black* and *male* as inherently contradictory, the fact of black abjection set irreconcilably against the anticipation of male privilege. This contradiction *should* be an opening to critique capitalism's persuasive ideology that reduces individual worth to monetary value. But as *Branded Head* implies, hegemony is in effect: even for men inhibited from achieving normative masculinities rooted in work, economic agency remains integral to their identities. Consumerism and commodification—brands and branding—thus become occult expressions of capitalist success that emerge as alternatives to conventional success within the labor economy. Through them, black men paradoxically are transformed into iconic figures of success within the fantasy of late capitalism.

THE EUROPEAN TRANSITION to industrial capitalism established a division of labor that assigned men dominant roles as "productive" wage laborers and left women to reproductive activities outside of the new market economy. Men's wages, in turn, enabled them to become providers—breadwinners in patriarchal, heteronormative households.

But while capitalism defined the laboring body as male, race placed black men at the intersection of male privilege and racial exclusion. To be black, as Cedric Robinson wrote in *Black Marxism* (1983), was to have "no civilization, no cultures, no religions, no history, no place, and finally no humanity that might command consideration." Black men had to navigate a contested terrain, struggling to assert their limited economic agency. Within the world capitalist system, then, black men were cast in three distinct but imbricated roles: as commodified bodies, as devalued laborers, and as fraught consumers.

In the slave economy, the black body was commodified both as labor (to produce value) and as capital (property itself). Blackness, in other words, was valued both as capital and subhuman capital-generator. Upon manumission, the symbolic weight of blackness did not just evaporate: black bodies continued to be subjected to the exploitations of the most degraded forms of capitalist labor, while the status of their humanity remained, for their white employers and coworkers, a question mark. Black men struggled to be paid wages equivalent to white workers and were frequently emasculated as "boys" at denigrating workplaces. And because this meant that black men did not center their identities around work, these jobs for the most part did not present themselves as obvious sites for black "working"-class struggle. Instead, as Robin D. G. Kelley shows in *Race Rebels* (1994), leisure, social spaces, and sartorial expression "enabled African Americans to take back their bodies for their own pleasure rather than another's profit." Unable to enjoy the social status of the (white) working man, black men survived and garnered status outside of the boundaries circumscribing "good" or "dignified" work. Opposition to economic and racial oppression on the job, in other words, centered performative expressions of black masculinity, and positioned black cultural forms such as music and style as important arenas of protest. Kelley illustrates this when he considers the political implications of Malcolm X's zoot suit. So, too, do Theresa Runstedtler in *Jack Johnson, Rebel Sojourner* (2012), her study of early twentieth-century world heavyweight boxing champion Jack Johnson and his cars and furs, and Mark Anthony Neal in *Looking for Leroy* (2013), his analysis of Jay-Z's self-branding as an "elite 'product'."

Naturalizing the masculine, and by extension *white*, character of virtuous labor was a hegemonic project, the ideological axis of economic domination. The theory of hegemony, developed by twentieth-century Marxist theorist Antonio Gramsci, explained how dominant group ideology transcends class to appear as common-sense understandings of the world and thus generate consent to domination. Stuart Hall adapted Gramsci's theory to describe how identity construction becomes "the 'trenches' and the permanent fortifications" of ideological struggle. Because various aspects of identity do not always align, they generate "contradictory forms of 'common sense.'" Hall was concerned with the clash of class and race in particular, a clash seen, for example, in white nationalist ideologies that produce antipathy to black and immigrant struggles, thus inhibiting the formation of a potentially formidable interracial working-class coalition.

But Hall's interpretation also illustrates the contradictions of black masculinity, an identity situated at the intersection of masculine entitlement and devalued blackness. Patriarchy, as a "common-sense" ideology, is a powerful incentive for black men to remain committed to tenets of masculine worth rooted in economic value—even when their devalued participation in the labor market means they are unable to achieve dominant masculinities themselves.

Striving to achieve economic value presents the aforementioned alternatives to labor: commodification and consumerism, *branding* and *brands*. Blackness, with its legacy of double commodification, is particularly susceptible to *disembodied* market value. Tokenism and cultural appropriation—valuable blackness coupled with the near or total absence of black people—exemplify the marginal position occupied by blacks in the marketplace. So while black laboring bodies in many instances have become redundant, the social registers of blackness have been converted into cultural capital and remain highly significant. Greg Tate writes in *Everything But the Burden* (2003) that, as capitalism's original fetish object, "the Black body, and subsequently Black culture, has become a hungered-after taboo item and a nightmarish bugbear in the badlands of the American racial imagination." The ubiquitous image of a dunking Michael Jordan hints at how iconic the black male body is in popular culture. Yet Jordan's repurposing as a commodity—one aimed at compelling consumption by other black men—renders his remarkable athleticism secondary to his power as a commercial object. This commodification of Jordan dramatizes the degree to which black manhood, so far as the market is concerned, has value mainly as a *trope*. Tropes, in this sense, are not only personifications of a stereotype. They are *performing commodities* that embody extreme expressions of livelihoods—whether celebrity or criminal—that are outside of wage labor and that are rooted in conspicuous consumption. For black men excluded from the labor market, such tropes stand in as promises of success in the capitalist world system. Indeed, for many they suggest an alternative to market fundamentalism: if conventional routes to masculine worth via virtuous breadwinning are unavailable, the freedom to make money any way possible and spend it with abandon emerges as a generalizable expression of manhood.

Like a blinged-out Horatio Alger, the black male trope is many things at once: as Tate maintains, the "ultimate outsider," yes, but also, as Nicole Fleetwood contends, "an ultra-stylish thug and the ultimate American citizen." In his essay "NIGGA: The 21st-Century Theoretical Superhero" (2013), Neal explains, "basic tropes of 'blackness'—black culture, black identity, black institutions—have been distorted, remixed, and undermined by the logic of the current global economy." This distorted blackness enables a "stake in transnational capitalism" but at the expense of being "posited and circulated as a buffer against white supremacy, political disenfranchisement, slavery, Jim Crow segregation and the collusion of racist imaginations and commercial culture." The commodification of blackness during a time when an ever-increasing number of the world's laborers are insecure, contingent, or chronically unemployed thus has the perverse effect of extolling blackness within the very system that objectifies it.

While blackness was initially subjected to what Aimé Césaire referred to in 1955 as *thingification* in service to capitalism, tropes of blackness now *personify* the ideals of making and spending—the basic freedoms of late capitalism. Even for black men who are never able to attain normative, producer-provider masculinities, the seduction of patriarchal privilege is a powerful driver. With their masculinities at stake, many seek out alternative means to demonstrate their economic agency. They achieve this by locating black value in its commodity form—*paying to advertise*, as Thomas aphorizes. Doing so enables black men to overwrite the dominant narrative of labor market exclusion.

Yet by accepting commodification as a source of black value, these strategies also perpetuate capitalist hegemony. The trope accepts the fundamental association of blackness with commodification as the cost of admission to the patriarchal political economic order. Just as the incorporation of blackness in the world capitalist economy reduced it to object status, black value thus recuperated is still—the more so, even—a product of racial capitalism. Resisting the denigrations of racial capitalism has become the means of its preservation.

IN 1961 Frantz Fanon wrote: "The economic substructure is also a superstructure. The cause is the consequence; you are rich because you are white, you are white because you are rich." We might also add that you are a man because you have money, and you have money because you are a man. It is in this context of unequal access to productive, remunerative labor that consumerism and commodification have become so pervasive to the public personas of black masculinity. From slavery on, the fact of *blackness* being the cause and consequence of economic devaluation has made patriarchal capitalist inclusion especially appealing for black men, like winning a rigged game against all odds. But in doing so, the terms of black liberation are collapsed into patriarchal entitlement and participation in capitalism, rather than being framed as a more ambitious anti-capitalist critique.

As a result of their structural position and the perspective it has given them, black Americans are in a privileged position to critique racial capitalism. But that is a potentiality, not a foregone fact. The risk of essentializing blackness, Hall warns, is that "we are tempted to use 'black' as sufficient in itself to guarantee the progressive character of the politics we fight under the banner." The cause may appear the consequence, such that all utterances celebrating blackness are treated as oppositions to racial capitalism. Among other things, this threatens to mistake consumer choice for social justice and branding for black power. A recent example is the controversy surrounding Colin Kaepernick's Nike contract, in which the terrain of struggle was in some senses transformed into one of brand visibility and consumer allegiance. Meanwhile Kaepernick's endorsement, embraced as a victory, overshadows the fact that his appointment as a Nike spokesperson in no way altered the fragility of black life in the United States—not to mention the debased conditions of Nike's sweatshop laborers abroad. Highly visible expressions of black masculinity—specious substitutes for revolutionary potential—thus become but a selling point for disposable bodies in the market of disposable consumerism.

At the same time that commercial culture converts black men into tropes, black men's purported deviances (as drug dealers, say) or deficiencies (as absent fathers) vis-à-vis the breadwinning masculine ideal are made—with equal parts disgust and fascination—the subject of exposés, white papers, and government programs. Initiatives such as Barack Obama's My

Brother's Keeper—which proposes that better mentorship, rather than structural change, is the key to black men's success—underscore the emphasis black respectability politics places on the *right kind* of remunerative strategies and consumption practices as the way to achieve black uplift. Such approaches have identified black capitalism as the source of black liberation. Beholden to the system, perhaps it is.

Yet for black people, "buying in rather than dropping out" acquiesces to "the link between commodities and identities," as Paul Gilroy observed. In other words, not all proposed routes to black liberation lead to the same place. Black *thingification* has the potential to be a powerful counterhegemonic force against the degradations of racial capitalism. The black radical tradition that Robinson outlined in *Black Marxism* understands anti-capitalism as an abolitionist politics—one that has the potential to benefit not only blacks but everyone ensnared by a global system of labor market exclusion and environmental devastation that will immiserate and finally destroy us all.

In the welcome resurgence of writing about racial capitalism, the integral role of patriarchy in upholding ideological and economic domination is often missed. But a truly radical counterhegemony can only be realized by disassociating *both* blackness and manhood from capitalist registers of worth. The original construction of the black body as a commodity object, after all, uniquely positions it to critique the commodity fetish. And likewise the contradictory location of black masculinity uniquely positions it to critique the patriarchal, heteronormative ideals of male economic entitlement.

Yet the trope—as the ultimate performance of black masculinity —has proven a ready proponent of capital. In *Black Looks: Race and Representation* (1992), bell hooks asks, "And what does it say about the future of black liberation struggles if the phrase 'it's a dick thing' is transposed and becomes 'it's a black thing?'" If this is the case, she warns, "black people are in serious trouble." True black liberation is rather, as Tate suggests, "divestment in the performance of 'Blackness.'"

Reproducing Racial Capitalism

Alys Eve Weinbaum

TODAY IT IS POSSIBLE for an individual or couple to purchase an egg from a woman living in, for example, Spain or Romania and have it fertilized, frozen, shipped, thawed, and implanted into the womb of a surrogate living in Mexico or Laos. Nine months later, they can travel to pick up the transnationally reproduced offspring, usually from a third party that has orchestrated this complex international exchange and reaped a substantial profit. After the market transaction, those euphemistically referred to as "intending parents," but more accurately described as "consumers," can transport their lively product to their home—in the United States, Canada, Israel, or elsewhere. Upon arrival it may live life no longer as a commodity but as a citizen.

The explosion of the transnational reproductive economy has been facilitated by two developments. As the flow of babies through international adoption has been staunched by national bans on infant export, people seeking to create families are increasingly turning to transnational reproduction involving purchase of eggs and gestational surrogacy. Additionally, proliferation of egg freezing corporations that transport cryo-preserved ova around the globe, on demand, has begun to eliminate long waits for eggs in nations that restrict their vending and donation. By 2020 the international assisted reproduction industry is projected to be worth $21 billion, with the U.S. sector cornering 30 percent of this market. The roughly 8 million babies born to date through in vitro fertilization (IVF) will likely be joined by millions more in the future. While multisite reproductive arrangements may not yet be routine, they are on the way to being common.

Transnational reproduction supplies what so many desperately desire. It allows for the creation of families, engineered through the careful selection of eggs and sperm, that *appear* to be genetically related. At the same time, it facilitates the flow of human capital and vital energy from poor regions of the globe to wealthier ones, from younger and poorer women selling reproductive labor and products to relatively older and wealthier individuals wishing to propagate. This economy—which many scholars regard as a key component of contemporary biocapitalism —raises a critical question: How have we come to imagine that the commodification of human reproductive labor and its various lively products is acceptable, even desirable?

Answering this question requires recalling the history of Atlantic slavery and its culture of slave breeding. This was, after all, the last time in modern history that human life was commodified through the express engineering and extraction of human reproductive labor and products. Enslaved women, often referred to as "breeding wenches," were used to reproduce more slaves. In this, they were compelled to reproduce not only their own kinlessness but also the economic system that historian Walter Johnson has dubbed "slave-racial capitalism." Above all else, the history of slave breeding compels consideration of the impress of Atlantic slavery on the cultures and politics of human reproduction in the context of contemporary global exchange.

Unfortunately, this perspective is largely missing from scholarship on biocapitalism, which treats specific dimensions of what Michal Nahman and Sigrid Vertommen call "global fertility chains": the use of biotechnological products such as IVF and the subsequent transformations in kinship, "oocyte vending" and the circuits through which frozen eggs travel, and gestational surrogacy in the Global South. Some ethnographic works—especially those focused on the Indian surrogate market (which was, prior to being banned to foreigners in 2015, the world's second largest after the United States)—attend to colonial legacies that continue to construe women in the Global South as natural resources to be mined and harvested. And yet, the relationship between four hundred years of slavery in the Atlantic world and present-day biocapitalism has gone largely unexamined. In drawing a connection between slavery and biocapitalism, I neither mean that contemporary egg sellers and gestational surrogates are slaves in any simple sense, nor that chattel slavery persists unabated or untransformed today. My point instead is that a powerful thought system brewed up in the context of Atlantic slavery and its culture of slave breeding has been repurposed to render *conceivable* (in both senses of that biologically laden term) the very idea of a reproductive marketplace in which in vivo practices and products are made available for purchase.

Consumption of eggs and gestational surrogacy to create progeny may not yet be mainstream, but the very existence of transnational reproduction alters a fundamental understanding of human reproduction —that it is free of market design. When one baby has a price tag, all babies may be commodified. When one woman monetizes her reproductive labor, any woman's eggs or gestational labor may be put up for sale. What I will shorthand "the slave episteme" thus persists, shaping the consumption patterns of those who purchase reproductive labor and products from the global marketplace. Of course availability of reproductive commodities follows demand. Bit by bit, the private choices made by individuals and couples are transforming the culture and politics of reproduction in which everyone participates by virtue of having been born to a fellow human being, whether to someone accorded the title "mother" or not.

BLACK RADICAL POLITICAL SCIENTIST Cedric Robinson's idea of "racial capitalism" provides a point of entry for understanding the endurance of the slave episteme. According to Robinson, Karl Marx and Friedrich Engels got it wrong. Racial slavery was not a precapitalist holdover, and the forms of racism that characterized the feudal world did not die with the emergence of capitalism. On the contrary, "racialisms," to use Robinson's term, have been continuously reworked over time in support of processes of extraction and accumulation, and, therefore, have been integral to capitalism over its *longue durée*. The violent production of inequality among human groups has always been what makes capitalism go, and the invention of race and the practice of racism have always been capitalism's favored engines of differentiation. Ideas of racial difference seamlessly facilitate the divisions of labor, credit, and conquest—and above all the distinctions between the "human" and the "less-than-human"—that rationalize ongoing dispossession.

And yet, to comprehend the impress of the slave episteme today, we must go beyond Robinson's account of racial capitalism. Crucially, what distinguishes slavery from all other forms of racial capitalism, such as colonialism and Euro-American empire, is that it was *first and foremost a reproductive enterprise*—both materially and ideologically predicated on the extraction of reproductive labor and products from the racialized bodies of enslaved women. As two generations of feminist historians of slavery have demonstrated, female slaves constituted the principal labor source of capital accumulation within the plantation economy. As field-shaping contributions by Deborah Gray White, Marietta Morrissey, Barbara Bush, Hilary Beckles, and Jennifer Morgan reveal, because women participated in not just one but multiple streams of labor—sexual, reproductive, domestic, and agricultural—their bodies and labor power were central to the maintenance of slavery. As Beckles lamented in *Natural Rebels* (1989), a watershed study of enslaved women in Barbados, the task before the historian of slavery is not the "absurd" one of adding slave women to the story of human enslavement in the Atlantic world, but rather of restoring history to those who constituted "the pivot" around which the entire slave enterprise turned. In the United States, enslaved women's pivotal role was thrown into high relief after the Act Prohibiting Importation of Slaves of 1807 forbade the international slave trade but permitted domestic slavery to endure. Forthwith, reproductive engineering became the only way, apart from illegal import, to procure new slaves. The racial capitalist logic of slave breeding is inscribed in planter's bookkeeping practices very clearly. As Morgan observes, planters recorded increase in slaves as capital gains alongside increase in cattle and horses.

Yet slave reproduction was not only a source of surplus value; it also had enormous ideological impact. As much as slave owners required women's physical labor, they depended on their symbolic value to rationalize enslavement. In slavery, "blackness" was not so much an accurate description of phenotype as it was an ideological rationale for women's enslavement: "blackness" justified slave women's use as reproductive tools, their children's status as chattel, and their own and their children's kinlessness. It marked the biological body and in so doing created the moral and social distance between black and white women that facilitated reproductive extraction and commodification. As a consequence, slave women's reproductive labor and products were thought to be alienable and fungible. After all, regardless of how white an individual slave might appear to be, she was, by law, too "black" to be recognized as the mother of the children to whom she gave birth.

As a process of racialization, slave breeding constitutes a conceptual antecedent for reproductive extraction in modern-day biocapitalism. Like the babies born to slave women, those born to surrogates are understood to be alienable—both rightfully and legally separable from the bodies that have labored to bring them into the world. Should a surrogate change her mind and wish to be declared the "natural" mother of the child to whom she has given birth, the law is not necessarily on her side: courts have been known to enforce surrogacy contracts, siding with those who have paid to have a child reproduced, especially when an embryo was created using some of the customers' own genetic material (sperm or egg). As disturbingly, the absence of international law governing reproductive exchange across national borders can protect consumers who find that the child reproduced to their specifications does not meet their expectations. This was in play in the so-called Baby Gammy case in which an Australian couple rejected a child with Down's syndrome born to a Thai surrogate. It was also in play when a baby boy was left in India when the intending parents decided that they only wanted his twin sister—as they reasoned, they already had a son. In transnational reproduction, it is possible for children to end up not only kinless, but also stateless.

Though the two are not the same, it is clear that Atlantic slavery set the stage for the reproductive body—its in vivo labor and its biological products—to be considered appropriate sites for capitalist investment and speculation. And, inasmuch as Atlantic slavery established reproduction as a racializing process, the connection between slave breeding and present-day biocapitalism raises a host of additional questions. Does biocapitalism also demand that reproduction function as a *racializing process*? More broadly, in what ways are processes of reproductive racialization rooted in slavery recalibrated today? To answer such questions, we must consider how racialization has worked to dehumanize laborers and thus to devalue their labor.

According to available data about those who work as surrogates or who sell their eggs, such reproductive laborers share economic need or precarity more than any one racial, ethnic, or national identity. In that sense, they comprise a truly multiracial reproductive labor force. This fact mitigates against the simple assignation of "blackness" or any other single identity to today's reproductive laborers. Static ideas of race—affixed to biology, skin color, ethnicity, or nationality—fail to account for the nuances of racialization at work in biocapitalism. Simply put, racialization in biocapitalism is a process inflected by a wide array of social and economic forces, including labor. Therefore, if we wish to understand the processes of racialization that shape transnational reproduction today, we must turn our focus away from the surface of laboring women's bodies and instead consider how reproductive labor (egg production, gestation, parturition, etc.), as work, racializes and in so doing devalues the work and the worker, as opposed to the other way around.

While in some cases work can bolster workers' perceived racial identities, in others it ascribes to workers the social station of a different race. U.S. labor historians Theodore Allen and David Roediger have shown, for example, that many Europeans—notably the Irish—were not initially seen as white (and were often depicted with "negroid" features and referred to by racialized monikers such as "smoked Irishman"). They only gained admission to "whiteness" by actively distinguishing themselves from blacks through participation in the suppression of black labor, including exclusion of blacks from labor unions.

Static ideas of race as something entirely inborn or biological do not account for the racial realignments that powered industrial capitalism. Neither can they account for the complex racial formations that power contemporary biocapitalism, whereby women across the globe are performing forms of labor inimical to the elite economic status of whiteness (even when they reproduce white-looking children for consumers). Put in general terms, static ideas of race foreclose awareness of the labor process as the origin of observable racial formations. They erase from view the interdependence of Atlantic slavery, colonialism, and empire—the intertwined systems of racialized extraction and dispossession that continue to uphold our global capitalist modernity. And, not least, they obscure the ways in which market-driven reproductive practices appeal to consumers by erasing from view the racialized thought systems (which are never the ideological possession of any single nation) that make reproductive extraction conceivable and thus practicable today.

THE COMPLEXITIES of tracking the slave episteme in biocapitalism are compounded when we consider that biocapitalism arose in the 1970s with the birth of the first IVF babies and the arrival of Big Pharma, and, crucially, at the same time as the economic system we have come to label neoliberalism. A product of its age, biocapitalism shares neoliberalism's calculating, obfuscating, and highly functional ideologies of color-blindness and post-racialism. Thus a final question: What has today become of the specific form of "blackness" that rationalized four hundred years of enslavement? Or, put differently, whither "blackness" in biocapitalism and neoliberalism?

For roughly four hundred years, the slave's status as chattel and thus her "blackness" was guaranteed by implementation of the doctrine of *partus sequitur ventrem* ("that which comes forth follows the womb"). This legal concept dictated that the child's status be determined by that of its mother, meaning that any child born to a slave became the property of the mother's owner, even if a slave's child appeared white (as was common in a culture that incentivized white men's rape of enslaved women). According to *partus sequitur ventrem*, a child born to a slave woman was always "black" and thus inherited the condition of enslavement.

Under biocapitalism, the slave episteme endures. The impress of Atlantic slavery is felt not so much through the specific exploitation of the descendants of slaves or of other black women, but rather through the racialization of the reproductive process that allows for the commodification of reproductive labor. For this reason, it is a mistake to affirm (or, for that matter, deny) the endurance of the slave episteme by pointing to (or, by searching in vain for) the reproductive laborer's visible "blackness." We must instead adjust our sights and ask new questions: How are processes of reproductive racialization transformed as they follow in the wake of globalization's obsessive international outsourcing in the name of lower costs and maximal profit?

To borrow the vocabulary of G. W. F. Hegel, biocapitalism *sublates* racial slavery, both negating and preserving it. It does so by erasing from view the ongoing centrality of processes of racialization, and by simultaneously devaluing racialized reproductive labor to make reproductive extraction conceivable and thus practicable. This is especially pronounced in our age of neoliberalism. Neoliberal ideology insists that the forms of racial power that were pervasive in slavery have become antiquated today and therefore irrelevant to the functioning of market relations. Yet forms of racial power rooted in slavery have been successfully recalibrated and once again set to work. Indeed, today they render in vivo reproductive labor the pivot around which biocapitalism turns.

Succeeding While Black

Keeanga-Yamahtta Taylor

MICHELLE OBAMA'S POPULARITY is a remarkable political feat. Her ascent into the public spotlight, after all, began as a receptacle of right-wing misogynoir. From the suggestions that she was ill tempered to the hideous portrayals of her as male or some kind of primate hybrid, Obama endured scrutiny unprecedented in the history of the role of first lady. This was hardly surprising given that the pageantry and pomp of the office had become synonymous with white and wealthy "ladies." Her opponents were quick to cast Obama—the dark-skinned Chicago native—as decidedly un-ladylike, characterizing her instead as an anti-American political militant.

Sensitive to these portrayals, Obama acquiesced when her staff asked her to soften her gestures and play down her political contributions to Barack's first campaign run. In her new book, *Becoming,* Obama describes how campaign aids encouraged her to "play to my strengths and to remember the things I most enjoyed talking about, which was my love for my husband and kids, my connection with working mothers, and my proud Chicago roots." Together, the Obamas became disciplined in responding to racist attacks to avoid playing into stereotypes. As Obama has famously said, "when they go low, we go high."

The strategy worked. A recent Gallup poll listed Obama as the most "admired" woman in the United States. *Becoming* sold a breathtaking 1.4 million copies in its first week, and its success is partly due to the perception that this is Obama's response to the years of silence—her chance to finally break free from adherence to the public rituals of U.S. power. And, indeed, Obama's book is her story in her own words—authentic and refreshingly un-ladylike. She endears herself to a broad audience as she freely recalls smoking marijuana with a boyfriend in her car, having premarital sex, living at home well into her thirties even after she was married, having troubles conceiving both of her children, yelling in arguments with Barack, and feeling bitter as she was expected to carry most of the burdens of her household after marriage. Free of the pretense often effused by those with wealth and power, Obama comes off as ordinary and relatable.

Obama describes the value of telling one's story this way: "Even when it's not pretty or perfect. Even when it's more real than you want it to be. Your story is what you have, what you will always have. It is something to own." For Obama, a person's story is an affirmation of their space in the world, the right to be and belong. "In sharing my story," she says, "I hope to help create space for other stories and other voices, to widen the pathway for who belongs and why. . . . Let's invite one another in. Maybe then we can begin to fear less, to make fewer wrong assumptions, to let go of biases and stereotypes that unnecessarily divide us." The root of discrimination, Obama implies, including the ugly discrimination she faced as first lady, is misunderstanding. Sharing personal narratives, then, offers a way for people to fully see each other and to overcome their differences.

This message has resonated widely, but especially with black women, for whom *Becoming* has been a source of pride and celebration. Black women have paid hundreds, sometimes thousands, of dollars to crowd into stadiums on her book tour, which speaks not only to the celebrity of Obama, but the depths of disrespect and invisibility that black women in the United States experience. Indeed, black women in this country are so debased and ignored that it often feels as if the success and public adoration of Obama can lift and make visible all black women—a sense Obama herself encourages.

Yet despite all the optimism and goodwill that Obama embraces and inspires, I find *Becoming* troubling. Sticking to her strategy for success, Obama reassures her reader repeatedly that she is not a "political" person. Instead Obama describes herself as a "child of the mainstream" who "never stopped reading *People* or let go of my love for a good sitcom. . . . And to this day nothing pleases me more than the tidy triumph delivered by a home-makeover show." But as someone who has been around politics since she was a child (her father was a precinct captain in the Democratic Party) and is now, domestically and internationally, one of the most well-known ambassadors of the United States, this denial is not modesty; it is misleading. Indeed, far from being apolitical, Obama is politically sophisticated, and any reader of her book should treat her that way.

Becoming, after all, is an exquisite lesson in creating ideology. As a political insider with broad pop culture appeal, Obama wields enormous influence in shaping discourse and opinion on critical issues concerning race, gender, public policy, and how we define progress in general. Lauren Mims, a former assistant director for the White House project Educational Excellence for African Americans, has even undertaken an initiative to create a curriculum for *Becoming* that she says will "disrupt the traditional practice of talking about black girls in pejorative ways and center them and their unique experiences to study how we can support them."

Obama, then, is not just telling stories; she is shaping our understanding of the world we live in, which is why it is so critical that we, as a public, interrogate her ideology. When we do, we might see that her story is not in search of the collective experience but instead celebrates personal fulfillment—the kind of self-involved, "live your truth"–inspired homilies that middle-class and rich women tell each other. *Becoming* normalizes power and the status quo while sending the message that the rest of us only need to find our place in the existing social hierarchy to be happy. This message is unfortunate because personal narratives—including Obama's—do have power. When stitched together and told honestly, they can create a map of shared experience that raises the possibility of collective action as a way to transform the individual circumstance. This is certainly true of poor and working-class black women whose personal stories expose the racism, sexism, and general inequality of U.S. society. These stories relentlessly pierce the treacherous idea that the United States is free, democratic, and just, and they prove the axiom of black feminism that the personal *is* political.

BORN IN 1964, Obama has no recollection of the political strife—including multiple uprisings in response to police violence and the assassination of Martin Luther King, Jr.—that unfolded in Chicago neighborhoods during her childhood. Instead, her memories revolve around her family's cramped apartment in Chicago's South Side, and her narration of her working-class family's history perfectly captures the systematic way that African Americans were excluded from the vast bounty created in the United States in the aftermath of World War II. Indeed, as a child, Obama was palpably aware that her circumstances were vastly different from those of the adults around her. While their potential was truncated by rampant racial discrimination, Obama was able to attend a promising new magnet high school called Whitney M. Young. She then went to Princeton University and eventually Harvard Law School, and by the mid-1980s, Obama was earning a six-figure salary at one of the most highly regarded law firms in downtown Chicago. By any measure, she and her equally successful brother, Craig Robinson, overcame circumstances that many of their peers inevitably succumbed to.

Racism does exist for Obama, but these two realities—the history of structural segregation that she and her brother emerged from and their subsequent success —shape her perception of racism as less an institutional phenomenon and more an unfortunate residue from the past. This does not negate its realness, but she sees its manifestation largely as a "deep weariness . . . a cynicism bred from a thousand small disappointments over time." She saw it in both her grandfathers, "spawned by every goal they'd abandoned and every compromise they'd had to make." It was why the neighbor had stopped mowing the lawn or even keeping track of where her kids went after school. And "it lived in every piece of trash tossed carelessly in the grass at our local park and every ounce of malt liquor drained before dark. It lived in every last thing we deemed unfixable, including ourselves."

One of Obama's best friends growing up was Santita Jackson, one of Jesse Jackson's daughters. In *Becoming*, Obama points to Jackson's talking points in his 1984 presidential run as an inspiring message of racial uplift. She writes enthusiastically about Jackson's national tour.

He toured the country, mesmerizing crowds with thundering calls for black people to shake off the undermining ghetto stereotypes and claim their long-denied political power. He preached a message of relentless, let's-do-this self-empowerment. . . . He had schoolkids sign pledges to turn off the TV and devote two hours to their homework each night. He made parents promise to stay involved. He pushed back against the feelings of failure that permeated so many African American communities, urging people to quit with the self-pity and take charge of their own destiny. "Nobody, but nobody," he'd yell, "is too poor to turn off the TV two hours a night."

Conversely, Obama saw how other "extraordinary and accomplished people"—including black women such as herself—had managed the skepticism they were surrounded by:

All of them had doubters. Some continue to have roaring, stadium-sized collections of critics and naysayers who will shout *I told you so* at every little misstep or mistake. The noise doesn't go away, but the most successful people I know have figured out how to live with it, to lean on the people who believe in them, and to push onward with their goals. . . . I'd never been someone who dwelled on the more demoralizing parts of being African American. I'd been raised to think positively. I'd absorbed my family's love and parents' commitment to seeing us succeed. . . . My purpose had always been to see past my neighborhood—to look ahead and overcome. And I had.

In Obama's telling, then, racism is not the defining feature of black life, and her profound success is a testament to the ways that striving and self-motivation make the difference between those who succeed and those who do not.

The absence of materiality in Obama's understanding of racism in contemporary life underlies her sharp rebuke of Reverend Jeremiah Wright. Known for his fiery sermons condemning the racism, militarism, sexism, and oppression in U.S. society, Wright became a thorn in the side of the Obamas during the 2008 campaign when it was "discovered" that the Obamas were members of his church. The media delved into his sermons and described some of Wright's incisive comments as "hate speech," which worked to fuel the presumed radicalism or militancy of the Obamas. The most widely circulated of these sermons showed Wright at his incendiary best:

> The government gives them the drugs, builds bigger prisons, passes a three-strike law and then wants us to sing "God Bless America." No, no, no, not God Bless America. God damn America—that's in the Bible—for killing innocent people. God damn America, for treating our citizens as less than human. God damn America, as long as she tries to act like she is God, and she is supreme. The United States government has failed the vast majority of her citizens of African descent.

In *Becoming*, Obama dismisses Wright's experiences and viewpoints as him "careening through callous and inappropriate fits of rage and resentment at white America, as if white people were to blame for every woe." She accuses him of viewing "race through a lens of cranky mistrust." Wright and older African Americans, she says, became "cranky" because of legal strictures of segregation that gave rise to a "narrow mindedness" in matters regarding race. Obama goes on to conflate the bitterness of older African Americans with the racism of older white people, such as Barack Obama's white grandmother who felt afraid of black men on the streets. That fear, she writes, "was a reminder of how our country's distortions about race could be two-sided—that the suspicion and stereotyping ran both ways."

It is a diplomatic reading—but ultimately a clumsy effort to reach across the profound racial division in the United States. Consider the political ramifications. By treating them as two sides of the same coin, Obama is equating African American anger—rooted in material deprivation and human subjugation—with white fear, rooted instead in racial stereotypes. These two worldviews are not the product of the same generational experiences, and reducing them to such forecloses the possibility that African Americans could ever find real redress to the inequality produced by centuries of slavery and legal discrimination.

Moreover, Obama's reading reinforces the perception that African Americans' persistent demands against racism are not much more than "crankiness" or complaining. When combined with Obama's own emphasis on striving as a way to overcome racial discrimination, this narrative reduces racial inequality to one of psychological impairment that can be overcome through sheer determination and a positive attitude. She fails to see how it was bitter struggle against real institutions that created the new world she was able to thrive in. Indeed, the Whitney M. Young Magnet High School that Obama attended was built on an empty lot that had seen multiple uprisings over the course of the 1960s. Those uprisings eventually caused the political establishment to acquiesce and take concrete steps to create a black middle class. Elected officials invested in schools such as Whitney Young while also exerting enormous pressure on the private sector to end the racial enclosure of segregation that had slowly suffocated Obama's parents' social mobility. The crucible of the 1960s widely expanded access to homeownership, college education, white collar professions, and formal entry into electoral politics for African Americans.

Obama was among the very few who benefitted from these transformations in the U.S. political economy. The short-lived reforms created by the anti-poverty programs of the 1960s lowered the rate of black poverty by expanding the federal bureaucracy and creating new job opportunities for black workers. But as the momentum from the political insurgency of the 1960s waned, political support for these programs evaporated. And as more time passed from the high point of the movement, the hardship experienced by most African Americans grew deeper. In 1964, the year Obama was born, black unemployment was 9.6 percent; by 1975, it had crept up to 15 percent; and while Obama was at Princeton University, in 1983, black unemployment inched up even further to a bewildering 20 percent—the highest ever recorded. Nevertheless, the successes of the few were held up as evidence that it was not the system that was broken; instead, black people simply were not taking advantage of all that the United States had to offer.

To make sense of the persistent low wages, housing instability, higher rates of poverty, and deepening social crisis that marred black communities, the political focus shifted violently to personal responsibility—or a lack thereof. In doing so, the infrastructure of publicly funded institutions—including public housing and other forms of social welfare—that had been slowly chipping away at inequality and poverty were dismissed as unnecessary and financially gutted. The picture of success for some African Americans—whether they were lawyers or young elected officials—and continued hardship for others created a distorted picture of black America. Like a funhouse mirror, it enlarged features such as personal persistence and responsibility while pushing others, such as the role of institutional racial discrimination, further to the margins.

Obama's book reflects this diminished view of public programs and the power of the state as a vehicle to create meaningful opportunities for African Americans. With the public sector out of view, her conception of social progression is freighted with "public-private partnership" ventures and mentorship steered by "gifted" individuals. Social change is thus based on the goodwill and interests of well-endowed funders and well-meaning individuals, while inequality is essentially accepted as something to navigate rather than dismantle.

IF THIS READING seems unfair, consider Obama's 2013 visit to Chicago's William R. Harper High School and her recollection of it in *Becoming*. As an institution, Harper stands at the intersection of racism, poverty, and violence. In 2012 twenty-one of its students were injured and eight killed from gun violence. Obama chose to visit the school in 2013 as she became increasingly focused on gun violence in Chicago. Just weeks before, a fifteen-year-old black girl who had just performed at Barack Obama's second inaugural parade was shot and killed in a South Side neighborhood a mile from the Obama family home.

On the day of her visit, Obama met with twenty-two students who had all been psychologically scarred by their constant exposure to gun violence. They related with frightening detail walking down the middle of the street to avoid stray gunfire and their routines of clearly identifying escape routes in case they needed to run. In the course of the meeting, one of the Harper students remarked to Obama, "It's nice that you are here and all . . . but what are you actually going to do about all of this?"

In her telling, Obama did not have much to say to them: "Honestly, I know you're dealing with a lot here, but no one's going to save you anytime soon. Most people in Washington aren't even trying. A lot of them don't even know you exist." It was an honest statement—one we are expected to read as refreshingly honest and "real"—but also one that betrayed the logical conclusions of seeing racism as a manifestation of psychology, bad intentions, or simple ignorance. When unmoored from the institutions of power and class domination, racism becomes impossible to address, combat, and dismantle.

In the book, Obama also recalls that Englewood (the neighborhood Harper is in) had been considered a "tough" area when she was growing up, but seeing the shuttered windows and dilapidated structures in

2013 showed how much more ingrained its problems had become. She blames white flight: "I thought back to my own childhood and my own neighborhood, and how the word 'ghetto' got thrown around like a threat. The mere suggestion of it . . . caused stable, middle-class families to bail preemptively for the suburbs, worried their property values would drop. 'Ghetto' signaled that a place was both black and hopeless."

But while white flight was certainly part of Englewood's history of decline, white people abandoned Englewood more than a half century ago. Englewood's problems of today are both historical *and* contemporary. The neighborhood has continued to suffer because successive city administrations have starved it and other poor and working-class black communities of desperately needed resources, opting instead to redirect those funds to whiter and wealthier sections of the city. In 2012, just months before Obama's visit to Englewood, Rahm Emanuel, mayor of Chicago and Barack Obama's former chief of staff, shuttered fifty-two public schools in Chicago—the largest simultaneous school closure in U.S. history. Meanwhile, Chicago has dedicated 40 percent of its budget toward policing.

Almost half of black Chicagoans between the ages of twenty and twenty-four are both unemployed and out of school. This economic situation *produces* crime, while arrests and imprisonment reinforce the tight circuit of oppression and brutality. There are estimates that 29 percent of black women in Chicago's South Side suffer from PTSD. These are material manifestations of racism, but Obama's telling treats them as sad but ultimately disconnected events that are the product of partisan politics, pessimism, bullying, even hate—nothing quite tangible enough to put one's hands on and dismantle.

Obama, who avoids any analysis of the systemic or systematic feature of racial inequality, offered the children at Harper this lesson: "progress is slow . . . they couldn't afford to simply sit and wait for change to come. Many Americans didn't want their taxes raised, and Congress couldn't even pass a budget, let alone rise above petty partisan bickering, so there weren't going to be billion-dollar investments in education or magical turnarounds for their community." In the end, she told them to "use school."

While the first lady of the United States does not hold a legislative position and thus is not able to secure funding for a school in need, Obama's normalizing gaze at inequality, almost accepting it as a fact of nature, reinforces the status quo for her largely black audience—and that is a dangerous proposition. Obama shows the extent to which she has given up on the idea that demands can be made of the state. These children don't have the luxury to "simply wait" for change, so their only option is to turn to their underfunded, lightly resourced school and work hard amid stray gunfire to get themselves out.

This lesson—that personal striving is an important remedy to racial inequality—is given a sunny, optimistic sheen when Obama tells us that local "business owners" later donated funds so that those same twenty-two Harper kids could visit the White House, meet Barack Obama, and visit Howard University. Obama tells us that her hope was for the Harper students to see themselves as college students and use that as motivation to change their lives. As she triumphantly declares at the chapter's end, "I was there to push back against the old and damning narrative about being a black urban kid in America, the one that foretold failure and hastened its arrival."

IT IS IMPORTANT to distinguish Obama's retreat to personal striving as not just the same old "respectability politics"—the belief that if African Americans just presented themselves as competent and upstanding citizens then they would be seen as entitled to the benefits of U.S. society. Even within the distorted framework of respectability politics, there was still an understanding of the materiality of racism, and there was a notion of collective endeavor—a "linked fate" among black Americans. In place of these politics, Obama concocts a kind of hybrid of middle-class feminism—with its focus on self-actualization, empowerment, and personal fulfillment—with wisps of J. D. Vance–style bootstrap uplift, which centers on hard work, education, and personal responsibility. By eschewing all "policy solutions," she sends a profoundly dangerous political message: that individuals alone can change their circumstance.

Indeed, in *Becoming*, she details her endeavors to bring poor and working-class children to the White House so that she could personally encourage them. There are multiple examples of Obama using the power of her office to pluck up black and brown students here and there to, in her words, say, "You belong. You matter. I think very highly of you." This is, without question, meaningful and valuable to the hundreds of young people who encountered Obama in person. Indeed, even the symbolic power of seeing a black president and first lady evokes the optimism that the Obamas often preach as antiseptic to the chaos of poverty. But, in reality, it also trivializes the enormity of the structural crisis and deprivation in communities such as Englewood. The crises in this country cannot be resolved one person at a time, and recipes for self-fulfillment cannot create the social forces necessary to transform neighborhoods.

In the period of struggle that bequeathed Obama the possibility of her improbable rise to the White House, Ella Baker, a radical black feminist and organizer within the civil rights movement, encouraged ordinary people to connect the dots of their oppression to a broader, unjust social order. Making these connections demonstrated the potential for an alliance of similarly aggrieved citizens and residents who do not benefit from our social order but suffer from its disorder. As she said in 1969:

> In order for us as poor and oppressed people to become a part of a society that is meaningful, the system under which we now exist has to be radically changed. This means that we are going to have to learn to think in radical terms. I use the term radical in its original meaning—getting down to and understanding the root cause. It means facing a system that does not lend itself to your needs and devising means by which you change that system.

The point is not to require from Obama a more radical viewpoint than she possesses, but rather to expose her ultimately conservative message. Obama served as an inspiring role model—her personal story is extraordinary by any measure. But it is crucial for both her and us to acknowledge that it was made possible by the confluence of institutional changes and her own talents. For the children of Harper High and their parents who live with PTSD and other scars of urban and suburban life in the twenty-first century, we must reaffirm our commitment to the same kinds of institutional interventions—and beyond—that made her ascent possible.

Another world is possible, but it can only be built through a collective struggle that Obama no longer sees as necessary.

Democratizing Elitism

Richard Thompson Ford

MANY AMERICANS think of college—and especially the selective university—as a social leveler, offering upward mobility to anyone with talent and drive. This idea helps to justify the stark inequalities of twenty-first-century capitalism: anyone, we are told, can ascend an eversteepening social and economic hierarchy and reap the growing rewards at the top. The elite status of the selective university seems available to all.

But, of course, it isn't. The result is that class stratification, cutthroat capitalist competition, and racial resentment collide in university admissions. Consider just the last year's worth of news.

First came the lawsuit claiming that Harvard discriminates against Asian American applicants. Strictly speaking, the suit made a specific claim of racial bias, but it was backed by a longtime foe of affirmative action and designed as a collateral attack on it. The case has fueled a more general critique of Harvard's admissions process by revealing the extent to which wealth and social status influence decisions.

Then came the "Varsity Blues" conspiracy to game the admission process at schools such as Yale, Stanford, and the University of Southern California, involving fake credentials and hundreds of thousands of dollars in bribes. To many this scandal is simply the logical extension of long-accepted practice: it is well known that rich applicants boost their chances with test preparation, application coaching, resume-padding summer activities, and family donations. An explicit quid pro quo, the argument goes, is just a more straightforward version of the same transaction.

Some view these cases as symptoms of the same disease: a shadowy admissions process that ignores objective merit. But this view misunderstands the essentially classist character of the modern elite university, in which race figures only incidentally. Far from providing grist for another argument against affirmative action, the bribery scandal in fact shows why it is justified. It also suggests that broader attempts to democratize elite university admissions are unlikely to succeed.

THE UNSTATED ASSUMPTION that folds affirmative action into a general critique of elite admissions is that acceptance should be based exclusively on individual merit (and that merit, in turn, should be measured by grades and test scores). Indeed, opponents of affirmative action often speak as if it is a departure from an otherwise even-handed and admirable meritocracy. But the Harvard case and the bribery scandal both expose—in high relief, if not for the first time—the extent to which non-racial (and hence legally unproblematic) admissions preferences dwarf those associated with race. Athletes, legacy applicants, and those otherwise likely to help universities secure large donations enjoy higher admission rates than members of underrepresented racial groups. Affirmative action is one of the more modest of many departures from numerical indicia of merit.

Critics also complain that elite admissions are secretive. But the real issue is not so much secrecy as indeterminacy: the process is fundamentally conflicted, relying on a hodgepodge of considerations and a mix of disparate criteria, rather than a single coherent idea of merit. This indeterminacy in turn piggybacks on the nature of the contemporary university itself, which is hardly a coherent institution with a single, well-defined mission. Instead it is an amorphous collection of distinctive, often unrelated, and occasionally mutually antagonistic enterprises. To have a clear sense of what a university should consider in admissions, one would need a clear sense of the mission of the university.

One of the university's aims—if increasingly crowded out by others—is the discovery and dissemination of knowledge. If this alone were the goal, admissions might be based solely on academic promise, which grades and test scores reflect in a limited and imperfect way. But this is not the only mission. To many, universities today are "supposed to be the engines of social mobility and the gateways to dreams," as *New York Times* columnist Frank Bruni colorfully puts it. This suggests universities should consider who would benefit most from admission. More prosaically, many universities manage several semiprofessional sports teams, for which they must recruit, necessitating a preference for athletes. And prestigious universities, in particular, have historically been finishing schools for the hereditary elite, a role that introduces criteria that favor the wealthy and powerful. This last role is distasteful to many, but it is hard to deny that it figures in elite admissions decision-making.

These roles can be complementary, but they are often in tension. The elite status that powers the "engine" of social mobility for the select few is in part a consequence of academic excellence. But it is also, in larger part, the result of networking with privileged young people who *already* enjoy the benefits of wealth and family connections. The effect of this preprofessional social networking—the chance to rub shoulders with and learn the habits, customs, and social mores of people whose success is guaranteed by their inheritance and their parentage—is powerful.

This elitism clashes with the idea of the university as a classless meritocracy, but it is indispensable to the status of the elite school and hence to the social mobility it offers. Consider a 2014 study that found that an elite college or university education has almost no effect on the later success of the typical well-heeled graduate: the children of privilege do no better after graduating from very prestigious universities than similarly situated peers who graduated from less elite schools. By contrast, a prestigious university degree does give a dramatic boost to black and Latino students and to students from lower-class backgrounds. The discrepancy is somewhat puzzling if the social mobility offered by an elite school education is a consequence of the education itself: one might expect a better education at an elite school to provide a greater boost to *all* students. But it makes perfect sense if the benefits lie largely in networking, socialization, and elite credentialing. The university has little to offer the upper-class student in terms of networking opportunities, acculturation to upper-class norms, and the imprimatur of the elite; she has these already by virtue of her social class. It is the lower-class student who stands to gain them by attending an elite university or college. This is not to suggest, as some have, that higher education is "worthless," even to people who are already privileged. It also does not prove that the education offered in elite schools is no better than in less elite schools. But it does suggest that whatever its superiority, it does not lie in instrumental career advantage. The competitive edge comes from networking, socialization, and the halo that surrounds an elite school credential.

As a practical matter, then, so-called merit-based admissions—however one defines merit—can only go so far: the children of the elite must always predominate if the school is to remain elite. A truly elite school admits the most talented student body it can *while still ensuring that most of the student body is drawn from the upper class*. If it were not for the American myth of the classless society, we could admit that an elite education is, among other things, a class credential. Elite admissions could then be understood as a ritual through which the upper classes sort themselves and decide which lucky members of the lower orders to admit into their ranks.

I should add that social class is not synonymous with income. Class refers to a culture and sensibility as much as it does to money. The families in the "Varsity Blues" scandal were all rich, but few were upper class: instead they were B-list actors and nouveaux riches professionals and financiers. For them, an elite school did not necessarily offer the prospect of increased wealth—indeed, most probably paid more for bribes than the education was worth in increased future earning potential. Instead it offered upward *class* mobility: buying a child's way into Yale is today's equivalent of a nineteenth-century industrial tycoon buying an aristocratic title.

THE IMPERATIVE to preserve elite status by maintaining an affiliation with the upper class is never stated openly. Instead, it most likely plays an unconscious role in informing whether an applicant will be a "good fit" or further the "values of the institution," and whether an entering class is a "good" one. All of this can be done without explicit reference to social class, because the idea of class is baked into the very culture of elite institutions: it is what gives them their character and makes them elite.

This fact explains all the preferences in elite admissions so many consider problematic: legacies; athletes who play expensive, patrician sports such as lacrosse, sailing, and crew; and, to some extent, the generic focus on well-roundedness, good citizenship, and personality, all of which have an unavoidable cultural and class definition. It is also reflected in the preference for applicants whose admission might inspire large donations to the school: here there is the direct benefit of helping to secure the donation, as well as the indirect but equally important benefit that such an applicant is almost certainly from an upper-class family. And last, this imperative to admit the upper class is reflected, of course, in elite schools' focus on high school grades and standardized test scores. Standardized tests predict nothing better than family income: the tests measure skills and knowledge reinforced in upper-class homes and private school. (When I took the SAT in the 1980s, one of the verbal questions was "scull is to river as car is to . . . a. garage b. brakes c driver d. asphalt." The correct answer, I believe, is d.) Moreover, reassuringly expensive academic test coaching promises to boost an applicant's score by up to 200 points, depending on how much coaching one "invests" in.

Grades and test scores get extra weight because of their importance in rankings, especially the *U.S. News and World Report*'s. High rank offers bragging rights and reinforces elite status. It is also self-perpetuating: because most applicants don't have the information or ability to distinguish between universities and colleges based on educational quality, many select based on rank. Of the many factors that contribute to a school's rank, the easiest for the school to control is the average standardized test score of its student body, so selective schools compete for students with the highest numbers. This provides an additional incentive for the universities to use test scores in their admissions decisions and to give small differences in scores more weight than their predictive value warrants. (The College Board itself admits that SAT score differences of up to 40 points should not be considered significant.) As a consequence, academic merit is taken to be synonymous with standardized test scores and grades.

Race plays a minor, incidental role in all of this. Until very recently, the upper class in the United States had been racially exclusive by design, and it remains overwhelmingly white. The imperative to preserve elite status by dint of affiliation with the upper classes introduces an indirect and inadvertent kind of racial disadvantage for non-white applicants.

This preference is indirect because it does not refer to race explicitly, and even most white applicants do not benefit. And it is inadvertent because the admissions officer is not deliberately trying to increase the number of *white* people admitted; she is trying, perhaps unselfconsciously, to increase the number of *upper-class* students admitted. From this point of view, affirmative action simply corrects for the unavoidable racial impact of a set of admissions policies that benefit the upper-class applicant. In this respect, the bribery scandal shows precisely why affirmative action is necessary.

The claim that Harvard discriminates against Asian American applicants is best understood in this light. If grades and tests scores were the only consideration, the number of Asian Americans admitted to Harvard would be much higher. But the data revealed during the Harvard litigation is consistent with discrimination based not on race, but on signs of social class. Because social classes come with distinctive cultures, signals of a particular class status may be considered virtues by many members of that class. Qualities such as well-roundedness, likability, intellectual curiosity, and leadership skills are unavoidably culturally specific. Thus, even if elite admissions officers are innocently evaluating applicants based on what they consider to be qualitative merits, they may be unselfconsciously selecting applicants who had best assimilated to upper-class cultural norms. And because Asian American applicants as a group do especially well on standardized tests regardless of social class, high test scores are more likely to align with elite social class for white applicants and less likely to do so for Asian American applicants. Class-based criteria were thus especially disadvantageous to those Asian American applicants who seemed highly qualified based on their grades and test scores alone. But such indirect class-based discrimination is not unlawful, and it is hard to see how it could be distinguished from legitimate qualitative evaluation as a practical matter.

WHAT IS MOST DEPRESSING about the latest conversation about university admissions is that it ignores all that is best about the university: its primary and most important function as a place of learning, insulated if not divorced from the profit motive. In our capitalist society that is driven by the bottom line, this is a type of privilege to be sure—not because it promises competitive advantage in a cutthroat job market or access to exclusive networking opportunities, but because it offers the luxury of intellectual freedom. This freedom contributes to new innovations and improvements in practical endeavors, of course, but these are often diffuse social benefits rather than individualized competitive advantages. Sadly, the exclusive focus on social mobility in the form of career advantage has all but eclipsed any discussion of these virtues.

The Harvard lawsuit and the bribery scandal will lead to calls for reform of the admissions process, and there is plenty to criticize. But much of the uproar has been based on unrealistic and even incoherent ideas about the nature of selective universities, their strengths, and what they can accomplish. The myth of the classless society allows the critics of university admissions to pretend that selective universities could somehow be less elitist but still just as elite. And this has meant that all the resentment over the classist aspects of university admissions has been displaced onto the relatively minor issue of race-based affirmative action.

The most sympathetic critics of affirmative action are really critics of the university admissions process more generally, but because almost all of what is most troubling about university admissions is perfectly lawful, the legal vulnerability of race-based affirmative action provides the only foothold from which to leverage attacks on the whole process. The strategy is confused and occasionally dishonest, but it is motivated by legitimate grievances. There is also a far less defensible impulse underlying attacks on affirmative action, driven not by concern for the white and Asian American applicants who are rejected but by resentment of the black and Latino applicants who are admitted. Class dynamics also explain this: hostility to affirmative action is often an instance of a characteristic U.S. antipathy toward uppity dark-skinned people who attempt to rise above their condition. What galls many critics of affirmative action is that it allows a smattering of black and Latino people to acquire an elite credential—complicating, if not exactly challenging, familiar racial hierarchies.

The discontent with elite university admissions reflects deep status anxieties and resentments, which, because they are suppressed and cannot be openly discussed, are unlikely to be resolved. It also reflects concerns over income polarization and diminished opportunities of success that public policy can and should address.

But fighting to revise selective university admissions policy is not the most promising way to address them. Greater investment in public universities, typically much larger and less dependent on elite legacy, might be more effective at promoting social mobility. Investment in economic development and job creation certainly would be. And to the extent that resentment of elite universities reflects legitimate resentment of elites generally, a more direct approach—such as taxation reform designed to reverse the polarization of income—would be far more constructive. The admissions scandals are a symptom of a society that pretends that elitism could be democratized—in which what passes for egalitarian struggle amounts to desperate individual attempts to ascend a steepening social hierarchy rather than a collective effort to level it. The demand for an equal opportunity to elite status is almost a contradiction in terms. A better egalitarian goal would be to level the social hierarchy that increasingly reserves a comfortable life to an elite few.

Michael Collins is Director of National Affairs at the Drug Policy Alliance.

Richard Thompson Ford is George E. Osborne Professor of Law at Stanford Law School. He has written for the *Washington Post, San Francisco Chronicle, Christian Science Monitor,* and for *Slate,* where he is a regular contributor. His latest books are *Universal Rights Down to Earth* and *Rights Gone Wrong: How Law Corrupts the Struggle for Equality.*

Helena Hansen is Assistant Professor of Anthropology and Psychiatry at NYU and a research scientist at Nathan Kline Institute for Psychiatric Research.

David Herzberg is Associate Professor of History at the University of Buffalo and author of *Happy Pills in America: From Miltown to Prozac.*

Peter James Hudson, Associate Professor of African American Studies and History at UCLA, is author of *Bankers and Empire: How Wall Street Colonized the Caribbean.*

Jonathan Kahn, James E. Kelley Chair in Tort Law at Mitchell Hamline School of Law, is author of *Race in a Bottle: The Story of BiDil and Racialized Medicine in a Post-Genomic Age.*

L.A. Kauffman is a longtime grassroots organizer and author of *Direct Action* and *How to Read a Protest.*

Julilly Kohler-Hausmann is Associate Professor of History at Cornell University and author of *Getting Tough: Welfare and Imprisonment in 1970s America.*

Jordanna Matlon is Assistant Professor at American University's School of International Service. She is at work on a book about racial capitalism and black masculinity.

Max Mishler, Assistant Professor of History at the University of Toronto, is currently writing a book about the intertwined histories of slave emancipation and penal servitude.

Donna Murch is Associate Professor of History at Rutgers University. She is author of the award-winning *Living for the City: Migration, Education, and the Rise of the Black Panther Party in Oakland, California*, as well as two forthcoming titles, *Assata Taught Me: State Violence, Mass Incarceration, and the Movement for Black Lives* and *Revolution in Our Lifetime: A Short History of the Black Panther Party.*

Julie Netherland is Director of the Office of Academic Engagement for the Drug Policy Alliance and editor of *Critical Perspectives on Addiction.*

Britt Rusert is Associate Professor of Afro-American Studies at the University of Massachusetts Amherst. She is author of *Fugitive Science: Empiricism and Freedom in Early African American Culture.*

Keeanga-Yamahtta Taylor is Assistant Professor of African American Studies at Princeton University and author of *From #BlackLivesMatter to Black Liberation* and *How We Get Free: Black Feminism and the Combahee River Collective.*

Alys Eve Weinbaum is Professor of English at the University of Washington. She is author of *The Afterlife of Reproductive Slavery: Biocapitalism and Black Feminism's Philosophy of History* and *Wayward Reproductions: Genealogies of Race and Nation in Transatlantic Modern Thought.*